30-SECOND
WINE

30-SECOND
WINE

THE 50 ESSENTIAL TOPICS,
EACH EXPLAINED IN HALF A MINUTE

Editor
Gérard Basset OBE

Foreword
Annette Alvarez-Peters

Contributors
Gérard Basset OBE
David Bird MW
Martin Campion
Jeremy Dixon
Paul Lukacs
Debra Meiburg MW
Jane Parkinson
Stephen Skelton MW

Illustrations
Ivan Hissey

IVY PRESS

This edition published in the UK in 2018 by
Ivy Press
An imprint of The Quarto Group
The Old Brewery, 6 Blundell Street
London N7 9BH, United Kingdom
T (0)20 7700 6700 **F** (0)20 7700 8066
www.QuartoKnows.com

British Library Cataloguing-in-
Publication Data
A catalogue record for this
book is available from the
British Library

ISBN: 978-1-78240-588-7

This book was conceived, designed
and produced by
Ivy Press
58 West Street, Brighton BN1 2RA, UK

Creative Director **Peter Bridgewater**
Publisher **Susan Kelly**
Editorial Director **Tom Kitch**
Art Director **Michael Whitehead**
Editor **Jamie Pumfrey**
Designer **Ginny Zeal**
Commissioning Editor **Stephanie Evans**
Profile & Glossaries Text **Jeremy Dixon**

Printed in China

10 9 8 7 6 5 4 3 2 1

CONTENTS

FOREWORD
Annette Alvarez-Peters

My journey to the world of wine began twenty
years ago when I was appointed to a beverage alcohol buyer position.
Though I was an experienced merchant, I had limited wine knowledge and
was facing an enormous learning curve. Determined to learn all that I could,
I was astonished at the range, and depth, of the many variables of the
wine industry. I not only needed to learn the business overall, but also the
important details surrounding soils, viticulture, vinification, grape varieties
and the regions they reside and a host of other fascinating disciplines.

In my early days as a buyer, I reached out to as many individuals as
possible in an effort to learn the business. The volume of information was
overwhelming and I needed to become a sponge to absorb the knowledge
available to me. I read numerous wine books and all the relevant trade
publications. I attended all sorts of trade tastings, harvest festivals and

visited many wineries. More importantly, I asked a million questions –
from the most elementary to the most insightful.

Throughout my travels, I've had the privilege of meeting producers both
big and small. Clearly the common thread among them is to produce the
highest quality wine possible given the incredible diversity of their vineyards.
As impressive, and educational, that these diverse wine properties can
be, it's the families and individuals that care for the land that are most
extraordinary. I am grateful to have toured vineyards and cellars and tasted
wines with some of the most notable producers such as Robert Mondavi
to Christian Moueix to Marchesi Piero Antinori. I have grown from their
generosity in sharing their knowledge and passion for wine.

Some of the best resources in my learning curve have been some of
the most accomplished and knowledgeable Masters; Masters of Wine and
Master Sommeliers. These Masters have spent years studying every facet
of the wine business from regions, soils, farming practices, grape varieties
to the foundations of retail and restaurant success. The Masters' abilities to
taste and evaluate wines are nearly supernatural. Gérard Basset is only one
of four individuals, worldwide, to be a Double Master having earned both
Master of Wine and Master Sommelier. Simply put, I was thrilled the day I
met Gerard. He is both brilliant and entertaining and exceedingly generous
in sharing the wealth of his knowledge of wine.

As a purchaser for a large retailer, I have the utmost appreciation for
consumers. A very important part of my wine journey has been observing
and learning about consumer behaviour . . . what influences their wine
buying decisions; What do they like to drink? How much are they willing to
explore? Today, consumers are rewarded with quality wines in every price
range. Furthermore, technology has provided unprecedented access to
information about wines from the world over, and wine lovers have never
had better tools to enhance their knowledge.

30-Second Wine is a perfect tool to help build knowledge and to discover
your passion for wine. Cheers!

INTRODUCTION

Gérard Basset OBE

Wine has a long, rich and truly fascinating history.

This remarkable beverage has quenched our thirst, heightened our passions and loosened our tongues ever since people in ancient Mesopotamia – or perhaps even before – first trod grapes and drank this elixir. Wine is the drink of conviviality, of celebrations, of success, of gatherings great and small; wine is sensual and sensorial. But why should the soil in a vineyard plot mean so much to the contents of our glass? What alchemy turns this juice from the humble fruit of the vine into a drink capable of being cellared for decades? While wine generates much interest the myriad grape varieties and wine styles can be bewildering and the language of wine can seem mysterious too.

30-Second Wine decants the subject, revealing the art and the science behind crus and clos, racking and riddling, and providing important insights into Burgundy, Bordeaux, Barossa, Tuscany, Napa and other leading wine regions, since fine wine is now produced in many parts of the world, from Brazil to China. This accessible book also gives a flavour of other intriguing aspects, including the various key factors that contrive to make possible the vastly different styles of wines – dark and tannic, fresh and light, bone-dry, nectar-sweet, sparkling or sticky – how the industry recovered from some seriously crippling events during its long history, as well as some unfamiliar details of the business of wine.

Compiled by wine experts steeped in knowledge of their particular field of expertise, this book allows you to master the art and craft of wine in 50 small sips – or rather, a mere 300 words and one picture. Divided into seven sections, the topics cover the essential elements of wine beginning, naturally, with **The Vineyard**. Section two, **The Winery**, goes behind the label and explains how wine is made, from the pressing of grapes to the method for sealing the bottle. The most important **Classic Grapes & Wines** – the so-called international varieties – along with the finest expressions those grapes are capable of producing form the subject of section three. Then follow the highs and lows of wine's chequered **History**. Section five gives a bird's-eye view of the **Iconic Regions**, from the centuries-old vineyards in Europe to

those of the New World that now hold their own on the world stage, and the potential of emerging economies whose wines are attracting increasing attention. The final two sections, **The Business of Wine** and **Enjoyment of Wine**, offer a taste of the ways in which wine is sold and consumed. The beauty of this book is that you can choose to read it from beginning to end or simply select the topics that provide the most interest to you, in the knowledge that any technical or unfamiliar terms are clearly defined in the glossaries. Finally, the people. The wine industry has produced a plethora of highly talented professionals, often entertaining characters. We have selected seven such personalities, all of whom have greatly influenced the course the wine industry has taken and had a major impact on making wine the magnificent beverage we can enjoy today.

30-Second Wine might simply enable you to join the discussion the next time you and your friends are sharing a bottle of wine, or it might fuel a new passion for this sublime beverage. In any case, we hope you will enjoy this book as much as the contributors have enjoyed writing it.

Santé!
Gérard Basset OBE

THE VINEYARD

AOC (Appellation d'Origine Contrôlée)
see appellation

appellation A system of labelling quality wine to reflect a legally defined geographic area of production. It is intended to offer a guarantee of origin and quality, based on such factors as permitted grape varieties, style and minimum alcoholic strength.

In France, where the modern-day appellation system was developed, AOC stands for *Appellation d'Origine Contrôlée*. At its heart is the notion of terroir. An AOC may be all-encompassing, such as 'Bordeaux', or more specific, such as 'Pauillac', which is a commune of Bordeaux. In Burgundy, AOCs even exist for individual Grand Cru vineyards such as Le Montrachet.

Other countries have their own systems, though none as intricate as the French. The equivalent in Italy is DOC *Denominazione di Origine Controllata*), Spain uses DO (*Denominaciones de Origen*) and Portugal *Denominação de Origem Controlada* (DOC). In the New World, the USA uses a system known as AVA (American Viticultural Area) while Australia has adopted GI (Geographical Indication).

Botrytis cinerea A benevolent fungus, also known as noble rot. It causes ripe grapes to shrivel and lose water content, thereby concentrating their sugars and other elements. Botrytized grapes are used to make sweet wines such as Sauternes or Beerenauslese.

clone A copy of a grape vine traditionally propagated from a cutting of the original. Clones today are more likely to be produced in a laboratory and grown for attributes such as their yield or for resistance to disease, pests, frost or drought.

IPM (Integrated Pest Management) An environmentally friendly approach to the control of pests, diseases and weeds. While it eschews use of agrochemicals, it is not as stringent as organic viticulture, but brings economic, environmental and safety benefits to the grape growers.

green harvesting The removal from the vine of a proportion of unripe bunches of grapes in order to concentrate the plant's energy on fewer grapes. Proponents claim the benefits include higher concentrations of sugars, tannins and flavour in the remaining grapes. Sceptics note that many of Bordeaux's greatest vintages predate the green-harvest fashion and were naturally high yielding.

late harvesting Picking grapes long after they reach optimum ripeness to achieve even higher sugar levels. The risk is that the crop may be spoilt by adverse autumn weather. Wines labelled Late Harvest are usually sweet wines.

The equivalent term in France is *Vendange tardive* and in Germany *Spätlese*.

lunar calendar In biodynamic viticulture the lunar calendar is used to time critical aspects of vineyard management including planting, weeding, harvesting and the application of treatments, and even cellar management up to and including bottling. The vine's four components – root, leaf, flower and fruit – are linked to the four elements of earth, water, air and fire. Each component is said to be favoured during particular points of the moon's cycle.

noble rot see *Botrytis cinerea*

Premier Cru, Grand Cru The quality classifications enshrined in the French Appellation (AOC) systems, but whose significance varies from region to region. *Cru* translates as 'growth' and can refer to a single vineyard or group of vineyards. On Bordeaux's 'Left Bank', only the five top wines are Premiers Crus Classés (First Growths). In St-Emilion, on the Right Bank, the top 13 wines are known as Premiers Grands Crus Classés with some 64 Grands Crus Classés estates ranked below them. In Burgundy and Champagne, Grand Cru ('Great Growth') is the top quality classification, followed by Premier Cru. Alsace has no Premier Cru classification

but around 13 per cent of its vineyards are classified Grands Crus.

rootstock The root of the vine on to which canes are grafted to produce fruit-bearing plants. Most rootstocks used today come from phylloxera-resistant, native American vine species or hybrids. *Vitis vinifera* is particularly susceptible to attack from the phylloxera louse. The most resistant American vine species are *V. riparia*, *V. rupestris* and *V. berlandieri*.

varietal A wine made entirely (or almost entirely, depending on local wine laws) from a single grape variety.

vigneron/viticulturalist One who grows grapes and attends to all aspects of vineyard management. An oenologist studies or makes wine. Since grape quality is key in winemaking, oenologists, especially consultants, are expected to have expertise in vineyard management.

vintage The grape harvest of a single year or the wine made from it.

Vitis vinifera The species of vine that is the source of most of the world's wine. There are many thousands of *vinifera* vines, all originally native to Europe and Central Asia.

TERROIR

the 30-second wine

RELATED TOPICS
See also
THE VIGNERON
page 18

TRAINING & PRUNING
page 20

THE START OF APPELLATIONS
page 90

30-SECOND TEXT
Stephen Skelton MW

3-SECOND SIP
Terroir encompasses the physical aspects of a vineyard – the location, altitude, aspect, soil – which together with local climate help define a wine from that vineyard.

3-MINUTE TOP-UP
Many explanations of terroir give the impression that soil type is responsible for 'flavouring' the wine, i.e. grapes grown on limestone will somehow taste of limestone. This has not been proved; there is no link between soil type and wine style and quality. However, differences in soil type, soil depth, mineral composition, drainage and water-holding capacity affect how the vine grows which in turn affects crop level, how the grapes ripen and thus the wine's style and quality.

The concept of terroir is one that underpins the Old World appellation system and is gradually finding favour in newer winegrowing regions. At its heart is location. Vines, although they may be of the same variety, clone and rootstock, will grow differently in different locations and the wine from those different locations will vary in character. Thus terroir is a shorthand way of explaining why all wines are unique. The vine is a sugar-producing plant and, subject to variety and wine style, the warmer the site the better the wine – within limits, as conversely, too much sunshine and excessive heat can give low-acid, flabby-tasting wines. Therefore, well-sheltered vineyards, at favourable altitudes and facing south in the northern hemisphere or north in the southern hemisphere, produce riper grapes with better flavours and more substance and body than vineyards that are cooler and less well-situated. Add to this equation – which starts with the natural elements that are unchangeable – man-made factors such as tradition, the variety and clone of the vine, planting density, pruning and training techniques and, above all, the yield of the individual plot, and the reasons why one wine differs from another become clearer.

It is now widely acknowledged that the nature and quality of a wine are – to a significant degree – defined by the place where the grapes are grown.

THE VIGNERON

the 30-second wine

3-SECOND SIP
Nurturing the growing grapes is the responsibility of the vigneron whose every waking hour will be guided by the quality and yield level desired to produce a particularstyle of wine.

3-MINUTE TOP-UP
For the vigneron, there are certain times of the year when a single event can ruin the entire crop. Frost in spring, hail during summer, fungus on leaves and grapes during the growing season, a starling attack just as the bunches are ripening, can all spell disaster. Whether it is lighting heaters against the frost, warding off hail by sending rockets into hail-clouds, spraying to prevent fungal diseases or erecting netting against birds, a vigneron must be constantly vigilant.

Demand for better quality wine

has refocused attention on producing premium fruit; no other factor is more important. The vineyard cultivator, or vigneron, manages all aspects of grape-growing, taking into account local climate and soil conditions, and is responsible for every decision that affectsfruit quality. This might include site selection, specifying the grape variety, clone and rootstock to be used, vineyard layout (whether up the slope or with the contours) and deciding on row width, distance between the vines, and the type of pruning and trellising systems to be used. The vigneron is also responsible for managing the annual tasks, from pruning in the dormant season, training the vines as they sprout their annual shoots, nurturing the developing crop, to ensuring that vines and fruit are not plagued by pests and diseases before the harvest. Additionally tasks such as deleafing the vines and crop reduction by bunch-thinning might be required. The vigneron will also tend the vineyard soil, cultivating or mowing the land between the rows and controlling weeds beneath the vines, even redistributing any of the precious soil washed down steep slopes by heavy rain.

RELATED TOPICS
See also
TERROIR
page 16

TRAINING & PRUNING
page 20

ORGANIC & BIODYNAMIC
VITICULTURE
page 26

THE START OF APPELLATIONS
page 90

30-SECOND TEXT
Stephen Skelton MW

The success of the annual grape harvest is a reflection of decisions made by the vigneron throughout the year as well as the vagaries of nature.

TRAINING & PRUNING

the 30-second wine

Vines are climbing plants and,

left to their own devices, would scramble over any available structure, seeking light and producing numerous tiny bunches of grapes. In order to produce the desired quantity and quality of fruit, commercial vineyards are arranged in rows for ease of access and harvesting, and growers have devised numerous ways of training vines on to trelliswork. Only rarely, in extremely dry regions (the island of Lanzarote, for instance), are vines grown unsupported along the ground. The aim is unchanging – ripe, healthy grapes – but training and pruning methods reflect climate, grape variety, wine style, regional traditions and legal requirements of the appellation system. Pruning takes place a month or two after harvest, when the vines are dormant. Cooler climates favour high-density, cane-pruned vineyards; warmer regions tend towards lower-density, spur-pruned vineyards. Cutting back to a small amount of fruiting wood curtails vine vigour, limiting yield and ensuring that the grapes are as ripe as possible. During the growing season, the vines are trained up trelliswork so that the fruit receives maximum light and air, although in very hot climates some shading is encouraged to prevent the grapes becoming raisins.

3-SECOND SIP
Vines must be managed – trained and pruned – to produce the right yield of grapes for the required wine: minute yields for ultra-premium wines; high yields for wines most people drink and enjoy.

3-MINUTE TOP-UP
Many factors determine how vines are trained, including the practicalities of working the land. On vertiginous inclines, as in Germany's Mosel, where tractor access is impossible, vines are trained on to single poles. Elsewhere, terraces are created on steep slopes to provide level surfaces for both vines and vehicles. On gentler gradients or flat land, higher-volume production is possible and vines appear in regimented rows, wide or narrow, depending on the equipment used.

RELATED TOPICS
See also
TERROIR
page 16

THE VIGNERON
page 18

3-SECOND BIOGRAPHY
JULES GUYOT
1807–72
French agronomist who devised the vine-management systems predominant in Bordeaux vineyards

30-SECOND TEXT
Stephen Skelton MW

Variations on two pruning methods feature prominently in vineyards: cane pruning, where the fruiting wood is held on long canes; and spur pruning, where the annual fruiting wood comes from a cordon of older wood and is held on short canes (the spurs).

1922
Born in Vosne-Romanée, Burgundy

1939
With both his brothers on the front line, he leaves school to look after his family's vineyard holdings

1942
Marries Marcelle Rouget, a winemaker's daughter, who encourages Jayer into viticulture

1942
Commences oenology studies at the University of Dijon

1945
Signs a 10-year contract with the Noirot-Camuzet family to manage several of their Premier and Grand Cru plots and make the wines in return for 50 per cent of the grapes

1945–50
Refines his winemaking techniques and sells his wines to négociants

1951
Leases vines in Richebourg, Vosne-Romanée and Nuits-St-Georges. Begins producing under his own label

1951
Buys, clears and replants part of the Cros-Parantoux vineyard

1953
Successfully lobbies the INAO to promote Cros-Parantoux to Premier Cru status

1970
Purchases the final portion of Clos Parantoux from Robert Arnoux's sister

1978
Produces his first 100 per cent Cros Parantoux wine which becomes a sensational success in the USA

1995
Last official vintage of Clos Parantoux made by Jayer

1996
Retires and hands control to his nephew, Emmanuel Rouget, while continuing to make the wine, plus his own Réserve cuvée, until 2001

2001
Passes responsibility of his vineyards to Jean-Nicolas Méo and the running of the Domaine to nephew, Emmanuel Rouget

20 September, 2006
Dies in Dijon aged 84

2012
Jayer's private cellar sold at auction in Hong Kong. Lot 98, just three bottles of Richebourg 1978, fetched HK$1,573,000 (£129,160)

HENRI JAYER

Henri Jayer gave the appearance of a modest Burgundian grower-winemaker, toiling in the vineyard and handcrafting wines in his modest cellar. Yet such was his following that when he died in 2006, every major newspaper from *Le Figaro* to *The New York Times* published his obituary. At auction in 2012, a case of his Vosne-Romanée 'Cros Parantoux' 1985 sold for more than US $250,000 (£159,140).

Jayer left school at 16 to help his father tend the vines while his brothers went off to war. In 1945 he signed a contract with the Noirot-Camuzet family to manage their Vosne-Romanée vineyards in return for a half share of the harvest. For the next few years he made wine and sold it to négociants, all the time honing his skills.

Eventually he inherited his father's 8.6 acres of vines in Vosne-Romanée, Echézeaux and Nuits-St-Georges and gradually augmented his holdings. His most significant purchase was part of the abandoned Cros Parantoux vineyard above the Grand Cru 'Richebourg'. Recognizing its potential, he cleared the scrub and boulders and replanted it with carefully selected Pinot Noir vines. It became one of Burgundy's most highly prized Premier Cru vineyards and was widely considered Grand Cru quality.

Jayer was well ahead of his time believing in minimal intervention in both vineyard and cellar. He was one of the first in post-war Burgundy to oppose routine chemical spraying and to advocate ploughing to control weeds. He also realized that low yields were the foundation of truly great wines long before that became the serious winemaker's mantra.

He believed adjustments in the cellar were unnecessary if the grapes were perfect and so he often discarded up to 20 per cent of his crop. He removed grape stems to avoid bitter tannins in his wines and was one of the pioneers of 'cold soaking' – macerating grapes prior to fermentation to extract more flavour, aroma and colour. For reasons of hygiene, he fermented in concrete rather than wooden vats and, to avoid stripping wines of character, eschewed the widespread practice of filtration prior to bottling.

Considered normal today but groundbreaking at the time, Henri Jayer's techniques produced critically acclaimed wines said to be among the most richly textured, complex and finely balanced ever made in Burgundy. Throughout his life he maintained a reputation as one of the greatest vignerons of his era and inspired countless others to strive for perfection.

PHYLLOXERA
the 30-second wine

Phylloxera vastatrix is the Latin

name of a destructive aphid, which in its root-louse form feeds on the roots of the European grapevine, *Vitis vinifera*, and over time so weakens them that they die. The aphid arrived in Europe from east and southeast USA, where it is endemic and lives on wild vines – American vines – which have developed alongside the louse and are therefore tolerant of it. At the height of phylloxera's attack, nearly all Europe's vineyards were affected. Despite desperate attempts to exterminate the pest, the only long-term solution was arrived at by grafting *vinifera* wood on to a rootstock developed from the louse-tolerant American vine, a practice now near-universal in Europe and elsewhere. Only in remote regions that have been isolated from the insect (Chile, for instance) are ungrafted vines grown on their natural roots. Grafting onto rootstocks brings other benefits, enabling vines to flourish in otherwise inhospitable conditions such as limestone-rich, saline or very dry soils, and in nematode-infested soils. However, growers in California who experimented with certain rootstocks tried varieties whose resistance to phylloxera was imperfect in their climatic and soil conditions and the bug was back, stronger than before, prompting a second epidemic there at the end of the twentieth century.

RELATED TOPICS
See also
A CENTURY OF CRISES
page 88

3-SECOND BIOGRAPHY
JULES-ÉMILE PLANCHON
1823–88
French botanist who first identified phylloxera

30-SECOND TEXT
Stephen Skelton MW

3-SECOND SIP
In the nineteenth century a small louse destroyed almost all of the world's vineyards, and it can still be a serious threat under certain circumstances.

3-MINUTE TOP-UP
Phylloxera (officially now called *Daktulosphaira vitifoliae*) is the deadly pest that brought the European wine industry to its knees in the second part of the nineteenth century but it is by no means the vine's only enemy. Two forms of mildew, downy and powdery, are ubiquitous, whilst spiders, moths, mites and bugs enjoy eating their way through grapevines, requiring vignerons to subject their vineyards to various remedies and treatments throughout the growing season.

The scourge of the vineyard: phylloxera remains one of the biggest threats to the health of the grapevine.

ORGANIC & BIODYNAMIC VITICULTURE

the 30-second wine

Organic vineyards rely on

naturally occurring materials – especially copper and sulphur – to protect vines against pests and diseases, and weeds are controlled by mulching and mechanical cultivation, rather than chemical herbicides. Synthetic fertilizers, fungicides and pesticides are not permitted. Biodynamic viticulture takes organic viticulture to a level higher, akin to homeopathic medicine, and follows the teachings of Rudolf Steiner, who advocated a 'whole-farm', self-sustainable approach to agriculture. It introduces the concept of self-healing by using certain preparations to stimulate the vine to produce its own defence mechanisms, including buried cow horn filled with manure or quartz, and composts that raise the numbers of worms and micro-organisms in the soil to aid root development. Biodynamics also encompasses the use of a lunar calendar, which is held to promote planting success by dividing the days into four types – root, shoot, flower and fruit – following the phases of the moon. Some highly rated vineyards have embraced organic and biodynamic principles and claim their wine quality has improved. Many growers follow a middle path, adopting Integrated Pest Management (IPM), which aims to reduce inputs by monitoring climatic conditions in order to predict diseases and the timing of pest attacks.

3-SECOND SIP
Organic and biodynamic viticulture eschews chemical treatments in favour of natural and mechanical solutions to pest, disease and weed control and naturally occurring fertilizers.

3-MINUTE TOP-UP
Vine-growing without the use of man-made chemicals is more difficult and often more costly than with conventional systems, but satisfies the desire to produce grapes in a more 'natural' and sustainable way that chimes with environmental and health concerns. Certified biodynamic producers include Huet (Loire), Cayuse (Washington) and Felton Road (New Zealand), while adherents to the biodynamic philosophy include Château de Puligny-Montrachet (Burgundy), Frog's Leap and Qupé (California).

3-SECOND BIOGRAPHIES
RUDOLF STEINER
1861–1925
Austrian philosopher, scientist and founder of the biodynamic movement

MARIA THUN
1922–2012
German biodynamic farmer and key figure in devising the sowing and planting calendar following the moon's phases

30-SECOND TEXT
Stephen Skelton MW

Belief that the moon affects life on Earth dates back to the observations of Pliny the Elder. Increasing numbers of growers are opting to work with rather than against nature.

THE WINERY

THE WINERY
GLOSSARY

barrel fermentation The process of alcoholic fermentation, usually at ambient cellar temperature, in small oak barrels. Wines fermented in new barrels (typically 225-litre capacity) have a better integration of oak flavours than wines aged in new oak.

blend The mixing of selected barrels or smaller vats of wine to create a larger, homogenous quantity. It can also refer to wine made from several grape varieties. Most wines are blends. Médoc claret, for example, often comprises up to four varieties. Non-vintage Champagne blends wines from several vintages. The French term for blend is *assemblage* or *cuvée*.

carbonic maceration A way of making red wine starting with uncrushed bunches of grapes. Fermentation begins inside each berry until carbon dioxide, a byproduct of fermentation, causes the grapes to burst, allowing fermentation to continue in the normal manner. The result is a more overtly fruity wine.

cooperage The activities and workplace of those who make and repair barrels and vats from staves of seasoned oak. Small barrels are often charred over a naked flame. The greater the charring the more pronounced the aroma and flavour imparted to a wine.

Eiswein/Ice wine A sweet wine made from late harvested, naturally frozen grapes most commonly in Germany, Austria and Canada. The frozen water content is removed after grape crushing, resulting in a wine of more concentrated sweetness, acidity and flavour. In the New World, ice wine is occasionally made from artificially frozen grapes.

extract A word used to describe the body or weight of flavour of a wine. Technically, extract is the non-volatile solids of a wine left after evaporation. They include sugar, acids, minerals, phenolics, trace elements, proteins and pectins. Wines that are not filtered prior to bottling are higher in extract.

extraction The process of drawing phenolics (tannins and colour) from grape solids into the wine during and after fermentation by various methods such as pumping over and pressing.

lees The sediment or solids made up of spent yeast cells and other residue of fermentation. Generally, a newly made wine is left to settle and then racked (drawn) off its lees into a clean vessel. A wine may be given longer lees contact for added 'yeasty' flavour, an example being Muscadet *sur lie* (on the lees).

maceration The steeping of grape skins and pulp in the grape juice or wine to extract colour, flavour and tannins. It can take place before, during or after fermentation and may be manipulated by temperature or agitation of the liquid.

méthode champenoise (Champagne method) A term which uniquely describes the intricate process of making Champagne. Integral to the method is that the wine is grown, made and bottled in the Champagne region of France. A landmark European legal case in 1994 ruled that no other region can use the term. Therefore, sparkling wines made in the same way elsewhere in France or Europe are commonly described as *méthode traditionelle* (traditional method).

must The sweet liquid that results from crushing of grapes prior to fermentation. It includes skins, pips, pulp and juice.

oenology The study of wine and winemaking. Oenologists also have expertise in viticulture, as grape quality is integral to wine quality.

oxidized wine Wine that has lost its innate fruitiness due to overexposure to air. Since the Middle Ages, sulphur has been used in winemaking to prevent oxidation. Controlled oxidation is part of the character of some classic wines such as Oloroso sherry.

remuage The French word for riddling, part of the Champagne-making process. Bottles are periodically agitated by hand or by machines known as gyro-pallettes in order to gather lees from the second fermentation in the neck of the bottle ready for removal (disgorgement) before the bottle is topped up with fresh wine, corked and secured with a wire cage.

tannin The drying, sometimes bitter or astringent element that forms part of the texture of red wine. It derives from the skins, pips and stalks of grapes as well as from the oak in which a wine is aged. Pigmented tannins bind with other elements such as potassium, calcium and tartaric acid over time to form sediment.

vat fermentation Alcoholic fermentation in large, inert vessels made of either wood, epoxy resin- or glass-lined cement tanks, or stainless steel. The French *foudre*, a traditional wooden vat holding between 20 and 120 hectolitres, imparts no perceptible oak influence to the wine even when new because of its relatively small surface area, compared to the volume of liquid it contains.

vinification The process of turning grapes into wine.

FERMENTATION

the 30-second wine

Louis Pasteur discovered the microorganisms that play such an important role in all life's processes. Before his time, wine was made by leaving grape juice in an open vessel and waiting until the sweet grape juice was transformed into an intoxicating liquor that sometimes tasted rather pleasant. We now know that yeasts convert the sugars in grape juice into alcohol, simultaneously producing the flavours that indicate that this is wine. Alcoholic fermentations generally rely on the yeast *Saccharomyces elipsoideus* used by bakers and brewers. While this might be described as the common yeast, many indigenous yeast strains are present in the atmosphere that are not good at producing an attractive wine, so the majority of modern winemakers need to add a specially prepared culture. The range of different strains is huge, allowing winemakers to choose whichever gives the style required. There are yeasts that help to make the finest fizz, yeasts that produce enhanced aromas, yeasts that encourage high or low alcohols – even very special yeasts that produce the most delicate of fino sherries. They are all pampered creatures, preferring warm conditions and plenty of nutritious food. Unless yeasts get what they want, they sulk and die, leaving the winemaker with a major problem and a tankful of half-made wine.

3-SECOND SIP
The miraculous transformation of grape juice into wine makes use of Nature's alchemists – yeasts.

3-MINUTE TOP-UP
There are thousands of different fermentations: some involve yeasts, whereas others harness the power of bacteria. Products of these fermentations range from detergents to incredibly complex pharmaceutical substances. Fermentations are going on around us all the time: from the conversion of garden waste into rich compost to the curdling of milk to make yogurt and cheese.

RELATED TOPICS
See also
FORTIFIED WINES
page 44

3-SECOND BIOGRAPHY
LOUIS PASTEUR
1822–95
French chemist and microbiologist

30-SECOND TEXT
David Bird MW

Accident, trial and error and advanced scientific knowledge have, over the centuries, enabled humans to enhance the metabolic power of yeast to produce a remarkable array of wines from a single source: fermented grapes.

SULPHUR DIOXIDE

the 30-second wine

Sulphur dioxide is probably the winemaker's greatest ally because it has many properties that help in the production of sound wine. But it is also the source of considerable controversy, as it is a rather unpleasant substance if misused. It has two particularly valuable properties, the best of which is that it is a powerful antioxidant and consumes oxygen very quickly. Wine is a somewhat unstable liquid, being halfway between grape juice and vinegar. Yeasts convert the sugars in the grape juice to alcohol, but bacteria then convert the alcohol to acetic acid, which is the essential base of vinegar. However, this latter reaction depends on the presence of oxygen, which is abundant in the atmosphere and will dissolve in wine – oxidized wine rapidly loses flavour, colour and aroma. This is where sulphur dioxide plays its most important role as a preservative, attacking oxygen before it can damage the wine, thus maintaining the wine in a fresh and healthy condition. Its second property, curbing the activity of yeasts and bacteria, is no longer as important as it once was owing to the development of modern bottling techniques. A small but significant quantity of SO_2 is produced naturally during fermentation by the action of yeasts on the sulphur-containing compounds in the grape juice.

3-SECOND SIP
SO_2 is the most widely used of the small number of substances that winemakers are allowed to add to wine.

3-MINUTE TOP-UP
Sulphur dioxide is a widely used preservative in many foodstuffs, including sausages and dried fruits. Winemakers of the increasingly popular natural wine movement eschew the use of sulphur dioxide, regarding it as an unnecessary additive, but making good wine without it requires very careful techniques to avoid dissolving oxygen from the atmosphere. European regulations require its presence to be indicated on the label because it is an allergenic substance.

RELATED TOPICS
See also
CLOSURES
page 48

WINE & HEALTH
page 152

30-SECOND TEXT
David Bird MW

A pungent, colourless gas seems an unlikely ingredient to find in food or drink, but sulphur dioxide has been used to preserve quality and freshness in wine since ancient Roman times.

MAKING WHITE WINE

the 30-second wine

3-SECOND SIP
White wines can be dry,
sweet or intensely luscious,
and sweeter wines are often
the best introduction to
developing an enduring
love of wine.

3-MINUTE TOP-UP
The world's great white
wines tend to emanate
from cooler climate regions
because white grapes
require less warmth than
black grapes to reach
optimum maturity. Also,
white wines need higher
acidity than reds to maintain
their refreshing nature
and acid levels fall with
increasing temperature.
Sweet whites need special
techniques, including
harnessing the ability of a
benevolent fungus (*Botrytis
cinerea*), the sun or even ice,
to concentrate the juice to
make gloriously intense
dessert wines.

White wine is usually made from white grapes, but occasionally using black grapes because most black grape juice is colourless. The simplest method is to harvest white grapes at optimum ripeness, crush and press them, collecting the juice for fermentation. The result will be white wine, but there are many refinements that can produce higher quality. Much of the grape's flavour lies in the skin cells, and unless these cells are broken the flavour is discarded with the skins. Luckily, the cells containing the flavour compounds are fragile and easily rupture if the skins are macerated with the juice, this process is known as 'skin contact'. Making white wine from black grapes requires a different process because certain skin cells contain colouring substances called anthocyanins, which, if the skins remain in the vat, turn the juice pink or even red. For example, when Pinot Noir is used to make still or sparkling white wine, the juice is separated from the skins immediately after the grapes have been pressed. Most – but not all – white wine is filtered for maximum clarity, although filtration can remove flavour as well as specks of solid matter.

RELATED TOPICS
See also
FERMENTATION
page 32

SWEET WINES
page 42

30-SECOND TEXT
David Bird MW

White winemakers begin with the same simple process: grapes are pressed to release their juice and strained to remove the solids. The juice is pumped into a vat, yeast is added and fermentation begins. Thereafter the options are varied because white wines run the gamut of styles from bone dry to syrupy sweet, from sparkling to fortified.

MAKING RED WINE

the 30-second wine

Red wines are always made from black grapes. There is no alternative because the red colouring material is found in the skin cells of these grapes, whereas the juice is usually colourless. Vinification also differs from that of white wine in that the skins are not separated from the juice after the grapes have been crushed, but allowed to ferment with the juice so that the cells become soft enough to rupture and release the colouring matter and tannins. This is a critical part of the process, and the winemaker's expertise is of utmost importance. Time and temperature have a big effect on the wine's style: too long a maceration will yield a tough and bitter wine; too high a temperature will result in loss of fresh fruit flavours. The fermentation temperature is generally higher than in white winemaking because of the need to extract the colouring matter from the skins, which is more efficient at higher temperatures. Fermentation is normally allowed to continue until all of the sugars have been converted to alcohol, with the result that the vast majority of red wines are dry.

RELATED TOPICS
See also
FERMENTATION
page 32

AGEING WINE
page 144

30-SECOND TEXT
David Bird MW

3-SECOND SIP
Red wine styles range from light to dark and fruity to heavy or complex and can be designed to be drunk almost as soon as they are bottled or built to last for decades.

3-MINUTE TOP-UP
In general, black grapes need more warmth than white grapes to reach full ripeness, which is why red wine production is more prevalent in the warmer parts of the world. Red wines, being vinified with the skins, develop powerful structure, flavour and texture from the tannins in the skins. Tannins need time to soften and to contribute to the wine's evolution, which explains why more red wines than whites are capable of improving over years – and tens of years.

The process for making red wine matches that for white, with one notable difference: the grape skins remain in contact with the wine during fermentation, which allows colour and tannin to be drawn into the wine. Most reds are vinified dry or fortified; the amount of skin contact determines the style: rosé or light red to dark and tannic.

MAKING CHAMPAGNE
the 30-second wine

RELATED TOPICS
See also
FERMENTATION
page 32

WHY CHAMPAGNE SPARKLES
page 86

3-SECOND BIOGRAPHY
ANTOINE MÜLLER
1788–1859
German cellarmaster who, with the widow Nicole-Barbe Clicquot Ponsardin, devised the technique of riddling

30-SECOND TEXT
David Bird MW

3-SECOND SIP
The world-famous sparkling wine produced in the Champagne region of France is made using specified grape varieties – Chardonnay, Pinot Noir and Pinot Meunier – and according to highly specified procedures but it is not the only wine with bubbles.

3-MINUTE TOP-UP
This method is used around the world, but it must be referred to as *méthode traditionelle* because Champagne-makers are very protective of their product. English sparkling wine uses this method, particularly successfully in southern England where the grapes are grown on Kimmeridge clay, the same strata that appears in the Champagne region.

The method known as *méthode champenoise* depends upon a fermentation in the bottle to produce the bubbles. The process starts with the production of a still, dry wine with all the grape sugars converted into alcohol. This wine is then bottled with the addition of a calculated quantity of sugar and some active yeasts. The bottles are then laid down in cold cellars hewn from the underlying chalk strata where they mature for at least 15 months (on the lees – the residual yeast) for Non-Vintage Champagne and 36 months for Vintage Champagne during which time the yeasts feed on the sugar, converting it to alcohol and producing the essential carbon dioxide that cannot escape. After maturation, the spent yeast has to be removed so that the finished wine remains clear when poured. Removal of this sediment is achieved by the complex process of remuage, or riddling, whereby small movements of the bottle gradually move the deposit into the neck of the bottle. By immersing the necks in a freezing bath, the deposit is trapped in a block of ice, which can then be expelled. The bottle is topped up with wine and a drop of sugar according to the style required, corked, labelled and sold.

Unlike table wine, Champagne is bottled before fermentation is complete. It undergoes a second fermentation in the bottle and the process of riddling, in which the bottles are given a slight shake and turned, helps loosen sediment thrown of by the second fermentation.

SWEET WINES

the 30-second wine

3-SECOND SIP
Sweet wines come in many
styles, from delicate and
elegantly sweet to rich and
heavenly luscious.

3-MINUTE TOP-UP
Sweet wine's most
important constituent,
apart from sugar, are the
natural acids that balance
sweetness with a sharpness
that refreshes the palate.
Certain grape varieties
possess this characteristic,
such as Chenin Blanc in the
Loire vineyards and Furmint,
used for the remarkable
Tokaji Aszu wines of
Hungary. The classic sweet
wines of Sauternes are
made with Semillon and
Sauvignon Blanc, both
recognized for their high
acidity.

Wine is sweet when some of the grape sugar remains in the wine after fermentation has stopped naturally or been stopped by the winemaker. This residual sweetness is tricky to achieve because wine yeast will continue to feed on sugar until it cannot convert any more into alcohol. Most sweet wines are produced only if the original grape juice ('must') contains more sugar than the yeast can consume. Sugar-rich fruit arises in several circumstances, the best being when grapes are attacked by a common mould, *Botrytis cinerea*, which develops under certain weather conditions. Rather than rot, the grapes succumb to what is called 'noble rot', slowly shrivelling into raisin-like berries, producing wine of incredibly intense complex aromas and flavours, with an amazing sweet texture. Sauternes, from Bordeaux's legendary Château d'Yquem, or Germany's Trockenbeerenauslese produced by Egon Müller estate are prime examples of these true marvels. Another way of concentrating the sugar is to allow grapes to freeze on the vine during a hard winter frost to make Eiswein. The frozen grapes must be picked early morning and pressed quickly while still frozen, the ice crystals effectively removing some of the water from the juice. Elsewhere, in hot climates, harvested grapes are allowed to dry in the heat of the sun, which gives the same result.

RELATED TOPICS
See also
FERMENTATION
page 32

RIESLING & SCHARZHOFBERGER
page 58

BORDEAUX
page 100

TUSCANY
page 104

30-SECOND TEXT
David Bird MW

Judged by their appearance, late harvested grapes may seem to be well past their best, but their concentrated sugars can produce sublime dessert wines; allowing the grapes to freeze is one of many ways of doing this.

FORTIFIED WINES

the 30-second wine

Fortified wines – usually of

15–20 per cent alcoholic strength by volume – can be made sweet, medium or dry, depending on when spirit is added to the fermenting must (grape juice) or to the fully fermented wine. Sherry, from Jerez in southern Spain, is the most complex because it ages under a veil of yeast, or *flor*, which changes the wine's characteristics while protecting it from oxygen. Most sherries are made from the Palomino grape – Moscatel and Pedro Ximenez are also used – and blended to a style ranging from sweet and viscous to delicate, bone-dry *fino*. In contrast port – synonymous with its country of origin – is always sweet because spirit is added much earlier in the fermentation, leaving residual sugar in the wine. Port styles are determined by the way the wine is stored. Ruby port resides briefly in large wooden vats before being transferred to tanks for blending. Tawny port undergoes maturation in small wooden barrels for 10, 20 or 40 years, depending on the style required. Vintage port is bottled after two years and then needs many more years in bottle. Other fortified wines include Madeira from the eponymous island (the best vintages of which are capable of being aged for decades), Marsala from Sicily, and Muscat from France (where it is called *vin doux naturel*), Australia and California.

RELATED TOPICS
See also
FERMENTATION
page 32

AGEING WINE
page 144

30-SECOND TEXT
David Bird MW

3-SECOND SIP
Fortified wines are made by adding extra alcohol, in the form of brandy or pure distilled spirit, to either 'must' or wine.

3-MINUTE TOP-UP
Uniquely among wines, Madeira is heated artificially or naturally over a long period to develop complexity and flavour. Originally Madeira, made from the Malmsey grape and fortified with brandy or cane spirit, was mere ballast in ships embarking on long ocean voyages until it was apparently discovered that the cask contents improved after undergoing the oven-like experience of twice crossing the equator.

Some of the world's most prized wines – sherry, Madeira, port and Muscat – are fortified. The advantage of fortification is that it produces wines that are stable and can be kept for several weeks after opening.

ÉLEVAGE

the 30-second wine

3-SECOND SIP
Otherwise known as 'raising up' or 'maturation', élevage is the process, after fermentation, that wine undergoes to bring it into the final state before bottling.

3-MINUTE TOP-UP
The final wine that goes into the bottle is a blend, even wine from great châteaux and famous domains. It will be a blend of wine made from grapes in different parts of the vineyard, perhaps from different varieties, using different vinification techniques, some from tanks to give freshness, some from barrels for complexity. The blender's skill is as important as that of the winemaker.

In modern wineries, most wines are fermented in stainless steel tanks, usually with automatic temperature controls. Sometimes the wine remains on the yeasty deposit (lees) in these tanks to develop extra complexity. But it isn't all high-tech: wooden and cement vats are returning to favour because their thick walls give good temperature stability, and one egg-shaped, cement design produces natural convection currents without the use of mechanical stirring. During this period there is an interplay between the spent yeasts and the wine's components that needs careful handling to avoid the production of unpleasant off-flavours. These reactions occur in anaerobic conditions – in the absence of oxygen – but this is not necessarily the optimum situation. Wine may be transferred to wooden containers to take advantage of the effects of gentle oxidation: the smaller the container, the greater the effect. The preferred wood is oak and its use has developed into a great art. Multiple decisions must be made regarding choice of oak and cooper (barrel-maker), whether to use large tanks or small barrels, how much toasting (charring) the barrel receives, its age (new oak flavours wine more than old) and how long the wine spends in the barrel. The winemaker's role is art and science in equal measure.

RELATED TOPICS
See also
HENRI JAYER
page 22

FERMENTATION
page 32

MICHEL ROLLAND
page 50

30-SECOND TEXT
David Bird MW

The choice of vessel in which to ferment and age wine divides winemaking opinion since the material used – oak (American or European), stainless steel, glass or, increasingly, concrete – affects the flavour of the wine within.

CLOSURES

the 30-second wine

3-SECOND SIP
For millennia cork has been the seal of quality for wine, but it can occasionally cause an unpleasant fault: corked wine.

3-MINUTE TOP-UP
The perfect closure is the holy grail for wine scientists concerned with cork taint and oxygen transmission rate (OTR). The new generation of winemakers can choose from a vast array of closures: natural cork of various grades; cork that has undergone manufacturing processes including one that was invented for the production of decaffeinated coffee; plastic stoppers of various designs; glass stoppers and screw caps. It's a competitive environment that ultimately benefits consumers.

A high-quality natural cork is considered the ultimate closure because it possesses the unique properties of sealing the bottle, while allowing easy withdrawal. It also allows the wine within to mature perfectly because the correct amount of oxygen can pass through the cork. The major problem with natural cork is the musty odour (termed 'cork taint') that sometimes occurs in wine. The bark used to manufacture corks can harbour the microorganisms responsible for this aroma, but on occasions the musty odour can derive from sources other than the cork itself. Production of plastic stoppers that guarantee there can be no taint was tried briefly, but these stoppers proved ineffective at preventing oxygen entering the bottle. Thus the screw cap – a perfect oxygen barrier – became popular, but it acquired an image of being a cheap closure and is still not universally accepted by consumers. In addition, after it was discovered that its oxygen barrier was too efficient, manufacturers had to produce a screw cap that deliberately admits a controlled amount of oxygen into the bottle. In effect, the situation has come full circle. The message in the bottle is clear: there's more to closures than keeping the wine from flowing freely.

RELATED TOPICS
See also
ÉLEVAGE
page 46

HOW TO TASTE
page 146

30-SECOND TEXT
David Bird MW

A decent bottle of wine can be rendered undrinkable unless it is properly stoppered to ensure its carefully made contents are delivered as the winemaker intended.

December 24, 1947
Born in Libourne, France

1965
Enrols at La Tour Blanche Viticultural and Oenology School, Bordeaux

1969–71
Attends Bordeaux's Institute of Oenology under Professor Emile Peynaud, 'the forefather of modern oenology'

1973
Buys into the Chevrier Laboratory of Oenology in Libourne; subsequently becomes sole owner

1979
Takes over Château Le Bon Pasteur on the death of his father Serge

1986
Begins his international consultancy at California's Simi Winery, after an introduction from Robert Parker

1988
Takes on his first client in Argentina: the Etchart family of San Pedro de Yacochuya in Cafayate

1992
Creates the first white wine made on St-Emilion soil in modern times, at Château La Grande Clotte

1997
Laboratory moves from Libourne to larger premises in Catusseau, Pomerol

1998
Embarks on his personal project in Argentina, El Grupo de los Siete, with Bordeaux wine partners

2001
Establishes Campo Eliseo in Toro, Spain with fellow luminaries Jacques and François Lurton

2004
Vilified in Palme d'Or-nominated documentary, *Mondovino*, which alleges his influence on the globalization of wine styles

2007
Starts The Rolland Collection, wines made from wholly-owned estates and joint ventures

2013
Named the seventh most influential person in wine according to the *Decanter* Power List 2013

2013
Sells his family's Château Le Bon Pasteur to Chinese businessman Pan Sutong for an undisclosed sum

MICHEL ROLLAND

Bordeaux-based, globe-trotting, Michel Rolland is arguably the best-known and most influential oenologist in the world. He has been pivotal in steering many of his region's greatest red wines, and their international equivalents, towards a consistently riper, more opulent and often oak-prevalent style.

Despite criticism from some quarters, he is in great demand, consulting to over 100 leading wine estates in 15 countries. Among them is the illustrious Château Ausone in St-Emilion; Pape Clément in Pessac-Léognan; Pontet-Canet in Pauillac and one of Italy's Super Tuscans, Ornellaia. He works extensively in California for several highly regarded estates including Harlan and Sloane Rutherford, as well as in Bulgaria, Greece, India and Brazil. Currently Rolland also owns or has an interest in ten geographically diverse wineries.

Rolland grew up at his family's Pomerol estate, Le Bon Pasteur, and, after graduating from Bordeaux's Institute of Oenology in 1971, first joined then – together with his oenologist wife Dany – later bought the Chevrier Laboratory in Libourne. Mediocre vintages in the 1970s galvanized Rolland into promoting his belief that meticulous attention to vineyard health and cellar hygiene could transform wine quality, even in lesser years. While most oenologists remained in their laboratories, he routinely visited clients, persuading them to improve standards.

By the end of the 1980s he was pioneering many of today's widely accepted practices. These include green harvesting, leaf plucking and late picking to obtain optimum concentration and ripeness of the fruit. In the cellar he enforced impeccable hygiene standards, promoted the benefits of new oak and became renowned for his ability to blend harmonious and complex cuvées.

Some critics argue his wines have a certain 'sameness' though the most prominent of all, Robert Parker, dismisses this as 'absurd'. While Rolland himself admits his preferred wine style is informed by his early love for wines such as Cheval Blanc 1947 and Latour '61, he is adamant that his objective 'is not to produce First Growths everywhere, nor to make identical wines all around the world, but simply to allow each wine to express the full potential of its terroir'.

CLASSIC GRAPES & WINES

1855 Classification A hierarchy of Bordeaux best wine estates drawn up for the Paris Exhibition of 1855. The rankings were based upon average market prices over many decades, and covered the red wines of the Médoc and the sweet wines of Sauternes-Barsac. The one geographical exception was the famous Château Haut-Brion, a Premier Cru Classé (First Growth) in the Graves region. The classification has remained intact for over 150 years, although in 1973 Baron Philippe de Rothschild of Château Mouton Rothschild was successful in lobbying for his estate to be elevated to First Growth status under a decree signed by the then Minister of Agriculture Jacques Chirac.

aromatic wine A wine made from one or more grape varieties known for their pronounced aromatic qualities. These include Muscat, Riesling, Gewurztraminer, Sauvignon Blanc and Viognier. Not to be confused with aromatized wine which has been confected with herbs, spices and other additives. (The Greek wine retsina has been aromatized with resin.)

backbone The term favoured by wine professionals to describe the tannic structure (or 'grip') of a red wine. The fruit is sometimes referred to as 'flesh'.

balance The overall harmony brought by the flavour and textural elements of a wine. To be considered well-balanced, a sweet wine, for example, requires balancing acidity; a tannic red, a certain amount of ripe fruit. If any one element stands out, such as excessive alcohol or searing acidity, a wine may be deemed unbalanced.

barrel fermentation The process of alcoholic fermentation, usually at ambient cellar temperature, in small oak barrels. Wines fermented in new barrels (with a typical capacity in the region of 225 litres) have a better integration of oak flavours than wines merely aged in new oak.

bodega A Spanish term for a winery, cellar or wine firm.

Botrytis cinerea A benevolent fungus, also known as noble rot (*pourriture noble* in French). It causes ripe grapes to shrivel and lose water content, thereby concentrating their sugars and other elements. Botrytized grapes are used to make sweet wines such as Sauternes or Beerenauslese. Botrytis develops naturally in certain vineyards in autumn, subject to the right weather conditions. In the New World, suitable vineyards are often deliberately inoculated with it for the production of dessert wines.

Côte d'Or A French *département* and the heart of the Burgundy wine region, comprising the Côte de Beaune and the Côte de Nuits. Its capital is Beaune.

green The term used to describe the unpleasant characteristic of a wine made from under-ripe grapes. In a white it may describe excessive tartness. In a red it may relate to a lack of fruit and/or an imbalance of bitter tannins.

international varieties The grape varieties that stem from the classic wine regions of Europe and are today grown through the wine-producing world. The top varieties are sometimes termed the noble grapes. Among the reds these are Cabernet Sauvignon, Merlot, Pinot Noir and Syrah/Shiraz. Among the whites, Riesling, Chardonnay, Semillon, Sauvignon Blanc and Chenin Blanc.

lees The sediment or solids made up of spent yeast cells and other residue of fermentation. Generally, a newly made wine is left to settle and is then racked (drawn) off its lees into a clean vessel. A wine may be given longer lees contact for added 'yeasty' flavour, an example being Muscadet *sur lie* (on the lees).

malolactic fermentation A secondary fermentation that occurs after alcoholic fermentation. Lactic bacteria converts a wine's harsh, malic acid into softer lactic acid with carbon dioxide as a byproduct. It is encouraged in red wines and in some whites. In regions where wines suffer from a lack of fresh, natural acidity, malolactic fermentation is suppressed.

The Médoc The best-known wine district of Bordeaux that extends north of Bordeaux city west of the Gironde estuary. It is often referred to as Bordeaux's 'Left Bank' and most famously encompasses eight appellations including the Haut-Médoc communes of Margaux, St-Julien, Pauillac and St-Estèphe. It was the first Bordeaux region to be subject to an official hierarchy of estates, known as the 1855 Classification, which is still in use today.

noble grapes see international varieties

CHARDONNAY & LE MONTRACHET

the 30-second wine

3-SECOND SIP
Chardonnay produces
some of the most elegant
and beloved wines in the
world, but suffers from
its affable popularity.

3-MINUTE TOP-UP
Dubbed the 'great white',
the Chardonnay grape
reaches its apogee in the
form of a few thousand
cases of wine produced
from vines on a small strip
of Burgundy named Le
Montrachet. This famous
slope has the ideal terroir:
mineral-rich subsoil, perfect
drainage and a sheltered,
southerly aspect for
day-long exposure to the
ripening rays of the sun.
The result is one of the
most complex – and costly –
dry white wines made
anywhere on Earth.

Chardonnay is the consummate politician. Comfortable in many guises, it readily changes its platform to suit its constituency and its flavours can range from citrusy green apples to buttery pineapple. Chardonnay's royalist home is Burgundy, where it is bottled under famed vineyard names, such as the revered Le Montrachet or, more populist, Meursault. The epitome of Chardonnay conservatism is Chablis in Burgundy's chillier north. Here the wines are fresh, vigorous and uncompromisingly austere. Chardonnay is also a key component in the world's finest sparkling wines, notably in the Champagne region where famed bubblies such as Dom Pérignon rely on Chardonnay to achieve their elegance and finesse. Dubbed the 'winemaker's grape', Chardonnay's generous fruit readily responds to winemaking techniques such as barrel fermentation, lees contact, malolactic fermentation or oak maturation. In the joyous revolutionary euphoria of the 1980s and 1990s, New World winemakers liberally employed all these techniques, each out-vying the next with overt, dolled-up candidates. Like any healthy political system, there is plenty of opposition and the reactionaries are now gaining momentum, especially in Western Australia, where unwooded Chardonnay has become a dark horse favourite.

RELATED TOPICS
See also
MAKING CHAMPAGNE
page 40

MEDIEVAL MONKS
page 82

THE JUDGMENT OF PARIS
page 92

BURGUNDY
page 102

30-SECOND TEXT
Debra Meiburg MW

It is almost impossible to find a winemaking country that does not produce outstanding Chardonnay, the most ubiquitous of all the white grape varieties.

RIESLING & SCHARZHOFBERGER
the 30-second wine

No grape matches Riesling for

its ability to reflect the terroir in which it grows or the brilliant cut and clarity of its wines. It is one of the most aromatic white grapes: peach, apricot, citrus, honey, herbs and (sometimes) a surprisingly pleasant petrol note, are identifiable, invariably balanced by exquisite acidity. Riesling is Germany's mainstay grape and its most famous vineyard, the Scharzhofberger, in the Mosel region, produces some of the world's most sought-after wines. Ancestors of the current owner, Egon Müller IV, bought this vertiginous slate slope in 1797 and its wines have unparalleled poise. Elegant, yet paradoxically concentrated, with a wonderful mineral backbone, they improve for decades. Scharzhofberger Auslesen can be incredibly sweet and packed with ripe fruit flavours. Eiswein, made from frozen Riesling grapes, and botrytis-affected Beerenauslesen (BA) and Trockenbeerenauslesen (TBA) achieve the same miraculous qualities with such intensity and complexity, they have been known to make grown men weep. While Müller's Riesling is considered the *sine qua non*, a handful of other German estates, such as J. J. Prüm, produce equally fine examples. In neighbouring Alsace, and Austria, Australia and America, the grape is frequently vinified dry.

3-SECOND SIP
In the pantheon of grape varieties, if Cabernet Sauvignon is the king, then Riesling is unquestionably the queen.

3-MINUTE TOP-UP
Egon Müller IV's wines command stratospheric prices: at auction in 2011, a mere 18 bottles of 1999 TBA achieved a record ¤5,300 (£4,200) per bottle. More modestly priced half bottles fetched a paltry ¤2,400 (£1,900). The wine has the viscosity of olive oil and a finish that lasts, literally, for minutes. Once tasted, it can never be forgotten. Riesling's many synonyms include Rhine Riesling, Johannisberg Riesling and Weisser Riesling. Do not confuse with Welschriesling – which is neither true Riesling, nor a grape grown on the steep slate slopes of Mount Snowdon.

RELATED TOPICS
See also
TERROIR
page 16

MAKING WHITE WINE
page 36

SWEET WINES
page 42

3-SECOND BIOGRAPHIES
NAPOLÉON BONAPARTE
1769–1821
French emperor who secularized many of Germany's finest vineyards

KATHARINA THANISCH
1865–1924
German widow who made the Mosel's first TBA in 1921

30-SECOND TEXT
Martin Campion

Broadly speaking, German Riesling is graded by ripeness of the harvested grapes, ranging from Kabinett, the earliest picked, to Trockenbeerenauslese, a late-harvest, nectar-like dessert wine.

SAUVIGNON BLANC & POUILLY FUMÉ

the 30-second wine

The classic home for this lively

green-hued grape is north-west France, where the river Loire lazily snakes across a flat verdant landscape polka-dotted with sixteenth-century châteaux. The districts producing the Loire's finest Sauvignon Blanc are Sancerre and Pouilly Fumé, and these geographic designations are proudly displayed on labels. Sauvignon has long been served in Bordeaux, too, but until recently few producers took it seriously. In Pessac-Léognan, however, Sauvignon Blanc grapes are fermented and matured in oak barrels and rank among the world's most revered. While Sancerre and Pouilly Fumé have long held sway with Europeans, it was New Zealand that put the variety on the global map. When pouring New Zealand Sauvignon Blanc, expect exuberant guava, passion fruit, kiwi and gooseberry flavours with herbal, grassy accents and brisk acidity. Other countries also welcomed this irascible sometimes grassy grape (Sauvignon derives from the French word *sauvage*, meaning wild): South Africa made a name for its Sauvignon by largely eschewing the green edges found in versions from New Zealand and Chile. Basking in the sunny Cape, the grapes produce a full-figured wine with tropical fruit nuances and high alcohol levels matched only in California.

RELATED TOPICS
See also
BORDEAUX
page 100

MARLBOROUGH
page 112

3-SECOND BIOGRAPHY
DIDIER DAGUENEAU
1956–2008
French winemaker who produced exemplary Sauvignon Blanc in the Loire Valley

30-SECOND TEXT
Debra Meiburg MW

3-SECOND SIP
Vibrant, zingy and bracing, the adjectives describing Sauvignon Blanc are anything but bashful.

3-MINUTE TOP-UP
In the mid-1980s New Zealand wineries such as Cloudy Bay produced a zinger of a wine that knocked the socks off the Loire Valley. However, maverick French winemaker Didier Dagueneau raised the bar by producing textbook examples of low-yield, barrel-fermented Sauvignon Blanc from the slaty soils of Sancerre and Pouilly Fumé. In terms of style, the world is again divided into two: those who love their Sauvignon barrel-fermented and those who prefer to leave its vibrant herbal fruit untamed.

The early-ripening, aromatic Sauvigon is the white grape of the upper Loire region of France and the variety that has become synonymous with New Zealand's output.

CABERNET SAUVIGNON & CHÂTEAU LATOUR

the 30-second wine

It's not easy being a king.

Cabernet Sauvignon bears the weighty crown of global adulation, but like any successful monarch, this thick-skinned variety has the loyal support of other influential members of the nobility: Merlot and Cabernet Franc. Dark-coloured Cabernet Sauvignon ranges from medium- to full-bodied, delivering sumptuous red and blackcurrant flavours accented with warm spice, tobacco, graphite and leather. Most wine regions warm enough to ripen it will grow at least a small amount of Cabernet Sauvignon, but its seat of power has always been Bordeaux's Left Bank, where this regal grape produces dense wines with crisp acidity and compact, linear tannins. In cooler climates this variety battles for ripeness and can have green, weedy aromas and intensely astringent tannins, but from warmer realms – Australia, California, Chile and South Africa – plush blackberry, mulberry and plum leap from the glass. Cabernet Sauvignon is also one of the world's most popular blending partners, used to give backbone to varieties such as Sangiovese, Shiraz or Tempranillo. Cabernet reigns supreme at the dinner table, where its tannins make dynastic alliances with fatty dark meats, such as roast duck, grilled steak or rack of lamb.

3-SECOND SIP
Renowned for its elegance and longevity, on its own Cabernet Sauvignon can be a demanding, tannic wine, so Merlot and Cabernet Franc usually step in to smooth its tough edges, rounding it out with gentle plummy fruit.

3-MINUTE TOP-UP
Cabernet Sauvignon is avidly collected by wine connoisseurs and reaches its apogee in Bordeaux, where it produces the longest-lived wines in the world. In a ranking of Bordeaux's wines in 1855, Château Latour was generally considered the finest wine of Bordeaux's Médoc area. It still is. Stern and austere in youth, this classic emblem of Bordeaux is fiercely treasured by wine lovers.

RELATED TOPICS
See also
BORDEAUX'S RISE TO PROMINENCE
page 84

THE START OF APPELLATIONS
page 90

BORDEAUX
page 100

WINE INVESTMENT
page 136

3-SECOND BIOGRAPHY
FRANCOIS PINAULT
1936–
French business and art collector, the current owner of Château Latour

30-SECOND TEXT
Debra Meiburg MW

Bordeaux's most famous red grape, Cabernet Sauvignon is equally at home around the globe from Barossa to Beijing, Chile to Canada.

PINOT NOIR & LA ROMANÉE-CONTI

the 30-second wine

Pinot Noir is as sheer as a

negligée and almost always pale ruby in colour when made into red wine: if you can see your date through the wine glass, surely you are sipping a Pinot. In wine terms, light colour is synonymous with light body and it is lightness that makes Pinot Noir such a versatile food match. Delicately perfumed with aromas of strawberries, red cherries and raspberries, Pinot Noir is matured in oak but always to add the merest elusive touch so that the wood never overwhelms the fruit. The temperamental princess of black grapes, Pinot Noir's colour, aroma and texture are greatly affected by vineyard climates and soils, so Pinot varies considerably from place to place. The ancient wine-growing district of Burgundy is Pinot's royal seat, its cool springs and warm summers providing perfect conditions for fussy Pinot Noir. While the grape has reigned supreme in Burgundy's Côte d'Or for centuries, it is also the backbone of France's famed Champagne district. Here, Pinot Noir's black grapes are harvested and crushed with the juice immediately run off the skins to ensure the wine remains clear-coloured – hence white wine from black grapes: Blanc de Noirs.

3-SECOND SIP
Soft red fruit, silky texture and perfumed with delicate nuances of violets, autumn leaves or leather, nothing's sexier than Pinot Noir.

3-MINUTE TOP-UP
Pinot Noir producers are an impassioned bunch and crop up the world over, seeking this holy grail of wines. Cool-climate sanctuaries in New Zealand, the USA and Australia produce sublime examples, but the most hallowed Pinot Noir comes from a few hectares in the heart of Burgundy owned by Domaine de la Romanée-Conti (DRC). Its most precious vineyard, La Romanée-Conti, grows the grapes that make the most exquisitely scented and textured of all Pinot. It is also quite possibly the most expensive red wine on the planet.

RELATED TOPICS
See also
MEDIEVAL MONKS
page 82

THE START OF APPELLATIONS
page 90

BURGUNDY
page 102

PRODUCERS
page 126

3-SECOND BIOGRAPHY
AUBERT DE VILLAINE
1940–
French co-owner and co-director of Domaine de la Romanée-Conti

30-SECOND TEXT
Debra Meiburg MW

Thin-skinned and fickle, Pinot Noir is the grape that seduces red wine producers the world over, bewitched by the peerless quality of truly great red burgundy.

SYRAH/SHIRAZ & HERMITAGE

the 30-second wine

RELATED TOPICS
See also
REGIONAL GRAPE
& WINE STYLES
page 74

BAROSSA VALLEY
page 114

WINE INVESTMENT
page 136

3-SECOND SIP
Not many varieties can wear two hats – let alone two names – but the mighty Syrah is not just any variety.

3-MINUTE TOP-UP
Oddly, top producers often chuck handfuls of white Viognier clusters into the fermentation tanks with inky, dark-purple Syrah. They insist Viognier softens Syrah and increases complexity. However, the maker of Australia's most iconic wine, Penfolds Grange, relies on Cabernet Sauvignon to give Shiraz added dimension. Widely considered Australia's most collectible wine, Penfolds Grange – dubbed Australia's 'first growth' wine – sources fruit from a range of South Australian vineyard sites and lasts for decades.

France's northern Rhône Valley

originally set the benchmark for fine-quality Syrah, a black grape the Australians adopted and, in a smart marketing move, dubbed 'Shiraz' a century ago. Their wines are distinctively different from classic Rhône style: Shiraz from Australia is a fruity, friendly, tail-wagging puppy of a wine; the same grape grown in France produces a more restrained, almost saintly, drop. The north Rhône is Syrah's spiritual home and the 120-hectare Hermitage its finest appellation; the wines seemingly live forever and tend to be lean and firm, with aromas reminiscent of smoked meats, leather, red berries and earthy black truffles. Down under, Shiraz is the Aussie flagship variety, its wines rich and spicy, with violet and wild black fruit aromas. Gutsy, meaty wines from the warm Barossa Valley, Eden Valley, McLaren Vale and Clare Valley set the standard. In cooler Australian sites, the grapes assume a gentle red fruit lightness evoking savoury dried herbs with peppery accents. The love affair with this deep-purple variety echoes in other wine-producing countries such as Chile, Argentina, South Africa, New Zealand and the USA assuming either name. Increasingly most label their wines Syrah, but occasionally a winemaker producing clean, fruit-forward, plush wine will don an Akubra hat and call it Shiraz.

3-SECOND BIOGRAPHY
MAX SCHUBERT
1915–94
Australian winemaker who created Penfold's Grange Hermitage

30-SECOND TEXT
Debra Meiburg MW

Syrah or Shiraz, depending on the latitude, is one and the same: the grape that makes some of the most dark-hued, full-bodied red wines in the world.

January 1948
Born in Wales, UK

1953
Emigrates to Canada with parents

1959
Moves to California with parents

1977
Gains a PhD in Genetics from University of California, Davis

1977–78
Postdoctoral Fellow, Department of Crop and Soil Sciences, Michigan State University

1978–80
Research Biologist, Stauffer Chemical Co., Richmond, California

1980
Works as assistant professor and researcher at the Department of Viticulture and Enology at the University of California, Davis

1986
Purchases property on Mount Veeder in Napa and moves there with husband Stephen Lagier, while continuing to commute to UC Davis

1990
Named Fellow, American Association for the Advancement of Science

1994
Plants first vines at Lagier Meredith Vineyard, Napa

1998
The Lagier Meredith Vineyard produces its first commercial wine

2000
Awarded the title of Chevalière de l'Ordre du Mérite Agricole by the French government

2003
Retires from UC Davis

2009
Inducted into the California Vintners Hall of Fame in Napa Valley

CAROLE P. MEREDITH

Carole Meredith is an American

grape geneticist and professor emerita in the Department of Viticulture and Enology at the University of California, Davis. During her research career she pursued several aspects of grapevine genetics, including genetic engineering and genome mapping. She is credited with discovering the history and place of origin of several significant grape varieties including Cabernet Sauvignon, Chardonnay, Syrah and Zinfandel – subjects of speculation for more than a century.

Traditionally, the identification and classification of grapevines belonged to the field of botany known as ampelography. It involves comparing the shape and colour of vine leaves, grape berries and their constituents. Since the 1990s, the study of vines has been revolutionized by DNA typing (or 'fingerprinting'), a field in which Meredith and her research team became world leaders. By extracting and manipulating the DNA from the leaves and shoots of vines, she was able to establish patterns unique to individual varieties.

Soon after this initial breakthrough, Meredith formed a multinational genetics cooperative (International Vitis Microsatellite Consortium) through which researchers everywhere could pool their findings on so-called DNA markers in grapevines. This led to an explosion of knowledge in grape varieties, their origins and inter-relatedness.

One of Meredith's early pronouncements was to confirm that California's Zinfandel and southern Italy's Primitivo were one and the same variety. In 2000, working with researchers from the University of Zagreb, she established this vine was also identical to a near-extinct Croatian variety, Crljenak Kaštelanski.

In 1997, with colleague Professor J. E. Bowers, Meredith revealed Cabernet Sauvignon to be a crossing of Cabernet Franc and Sauvignon Blanc. This discovery was followed by the revelation that Pinot Noir had parented no fewer than 16 well-known grape varieties. Its offspring include Chardonnay, the Gamay grape of Beaujolais and Muscadet's Melon de Bourgogne. Publication of these findings in 1999, in the prestigious journal *Science*, reflects their importance to the scientific community at large.

As well as being historically intriguing to serious wine lovers everywhere, Meredith's pioneering research has practical implications for the conservation of grape varieties and for avoiding genetic inbreeding among vines. It has broadened the horizons for grapevine breeders aiming to develop new varieties resistant to pests, diseases and even adverse climatic conditions.

Meredith retired from academia in 2003 to devote more time to her wine estate, which she owns with her husband Stephen Lagier in the Mount Veeder district of Napa Valley.

TEMPRANILLO & RIBERA DEL DUERO

the 30-second wine

3-SECOND SIP
An easy-drinking wine compatible with a range of foods, Tempranillo may be the gem of Spanish viticulture but it is one of Australia's fastest-emerging varieties.

3-MINUTE TOP-UP
Tempranillo assumes more aliases than an MI5 agent. The grape has about 15 pseudonyms in Spain alone, ranging from the straightforward Tinto Fino in Ribera del Duero to the tongue-twisting Ull de Llebre (eye of the hare) in Catalonia. In port wines, Tempranillo assumes the name Tinta Roriz. Perhaps Tempranillo has such a long list of aliases because it is not an easy grape to pin down. Descriptions such as strawberry, plum and tobacco leaf are helpful but limited.

Tempranillo is such an early-ripening grape that its name was coined from the Spanish word for 'early': *temprano*. Its wine sings with red fruit and has silky tannins, similar to Pinot Noir, but with soft, gentle acidity. Inseparable from Spain, Tempranillo is so ubiquitous in the Spanish landscape that one is hard-pressed to find a region without this affable vine. Across the grape's northern stronghold Rioja and Ribera del Duero stand out – both regions produce long-lived, high-quality Tempranillo. In Rioja, source of Spain's best-known red wine, Tempranillo is dominant, usually topped up with two other varieties, Grenache and Carignan, and tends to be lighter-bodied than wines from Ribera del Duero, which are more dense, tannic and powerful. Ribera's – and Spain's – most revered wine is Vega Sicilia's Unico, a stunning Tempranillo backed by Cabernet Sauvignon. A thirsty public must also be patient: the lush, elegant, spicy wine from this 150-year-old bodega is aged for at least a decade in barrel and bottle before its release. Spain's penchant for maturing Tempranillo in American oak integrates vanilla and coconut aromas into the wine, bringing to mind a strawberry-vanilla ice lolly. With age comes reverence: Tempranillo develops a complex leather and autumnal bouquet.

RELATED TOPICS
See also
REGIONAL GRAPES
& WINE STYLES
page 74

RIOJA
page 108

WINE INVESTMENT
page 136

3-SECOND BIOGRAPHY
PABLO ALVAREZ
fl. 1982
Unassuming General Director of Vegas Sicilia and producer of Unico, a tempranillo blend widely revered as Spain's finest wine

30-SECOND TEXT
Debra Meiburg MW

Vibrant, savoury Tempranillo, once a local hero of northern Spain, has now become a major player on the international wine scene.

NEBBIOLO & BAROLO

the 30-second wine

Three years before Kublai Khan

founded the Yuan dynasty, writers were praising the Nebbiolo grape of northern Italy's Piemonte region. Described as *nibiol* in 1268, its name is based on the Latin root *nebula*, meaning 'fog' or 'mist'. Most authorities believe it is known as the 'fog grape' because it ripens significantly later than other red varieties – not until late September and October when autumnal mists shroud Piemonte's hills and the white truffle season begins. Light-hued Nebbiolo is often compared to Pinot Noir as both are notoriously finicky, site-sensitive varieties. But when the gods align, their haunting aromas and ethereal elegance are unmatched in the wine world. Unlike Pinot Noir, Nebbiolo has had limited success outside its ancestral home. Winemakers in California, Australia, Chile and Argentina have fussed and fiddled with the grape, but it never reaches the glorious complexity and regal bearing of Piemonte's top sites, Barolo and Barbaresco. Youthful Nebbiolo is obdurately tannic and acidic, but after a decade or more its tannins have matured to a soft dustiness. Unquestionably Giacomo Conterno reigns supreme as Piemonte's winemaker producing iconic Barolo, an exquisite wine derived from the cluster of villages oft-cited as producing 'the wine of kings and the king of wines'.

RELATED TOPICS
See also
TUSCANY
page 104

3-SECOND BIOGRAPHY
GIACOMO CONTERNO
1895–1971
Italian grape grower and producer and one of the first to bottle his own Barolo

30-SECOND TEXT
Debra Meiburg MW

3-SECOND SIP
Nebbiolo tantalizes with an exotic array of cherry and damson fruit, aniseed, dried herbs or liquorice spices, and an earthiness reminiscent of truffles, leather and tar.

3-MINUTE TOP-UP
This ancient variety was so greatly prized in Piemonte that a series of penalties was devised to deter ambitious neighbours from pilfering cuttings. In the fifteenth century, the statutes of La Morra village ordered a five-lire fine levied on sneaks who pirated Nebbiolo vine cuttings. A few pages later, the statutes prescribed lopping off the hands of repeat offenders, with hanging recommended for unapologetic looters who damaged more than fifteen vines.

Quintessentially Italian, Nebbiolo is rarely seen beyond Piemonte where, in the right hands, it produces some of the slowest-maturing of all red wines with the haunting aromas of its hilltop home.

REGIONAL GRAPES & WINE STYLES

the 30-second wine

RELATED TOPICS
See also
TERROIR
page 16

THE START OF APPELLATIONS
page 90

HOW TO TASTE
page 146

FOOD & WINE
page 148

30-SECOND TEXT
Debra Meiburg MW

3-SECOND SIP
Grape variety, geographical location and alcohol levels largely determine style but all wines can be loosely divided into light-, medium- or full-bodied.

3-MINUTE TOP-UP
Fat, round or lean, we're all obsessed with body image. Just like humans, wine comes in different weights or styles but it is important that the weight is in balance with its fruity character, acidity, sweetness and alcohol content. Without sufficient flavour to round out the delicacy, however, the wine is disparagingly described as thin.

Beyond the familiar 'international' grapes are regional varieties, historically rooted to a place and adapted to its terroir. Appellation laws specified which grapes could be planted to preserve a wine's identity – so Hungary's Tokaji must be made with the Furmint grape and Stellenbosch red Cape Blends always include the distinctively South African Pinotage. Variety primarily determines a wine's weight or style, but location is important. Warm climates produce high-alcohol wines and typically reds from such climes are full-bodied, heavy, dark-hued with concentrated fruit: consider Malbec (Argentina), Zinfandel (California), Aglianico (Italy), Carmenere (Chile), Mourvedre and Tannat (southern France). Cooler climates normally yield lightly pigmented grapes, hence lighter-bodied, delicate wines such as Italy's Bardolino from Corvina and Rondinella grapes grown beneath the alpine foothills. Light white wines, pale as water, are easily spotted and include Pinot Grigio (Italy), Chenin Blanc (France, South Africa), Albarino, Verdehlo (Spain) and Torrontes (Argentina). Medium-weight whites encompass delicate and floral Arneis (Italy), Assyrtiko (Greece) and savoury Grüner Veltliner (Austria). Apricot-scented Viognier (France, New Zealand, USA) is a full-bodied white grape, but the white heavyweight champion is an aromatic globetrotter: Gewurztraminer.

From Assyrtiko to Zinfandel, the array of hundreds of grape varieties is at once exciting and daunting, although all wines can be more readily identified by their style.

HISTORY

1855 Classification A hierarchy of Bordeaux best wine estates drawn up for the Paris Exhibition of 1855. The rankings were based upon average market prices over many decades, and therefore covered the red wines of the Médoc and the sweet wines of Sauternes-Barsac. The one geographical exception was the famous Château Haut-Brion, a Premier Cru Classé (First Growth) in the Graves region. The classification has remained intact for over 150 years, although in 1973 Baron Philippe de Rothschild of Château Mouton Rothschild was successful in lobbying for his estate to be elevated to First Growth status under a decree signed by the then Minister of Agriculture Jacques Chirac.

blind tasting An objective form of wine tasting in which participants assess the quality of a wine, and in some instances try to determine its precise origin, without knowing its identity. Its prime benefit is to eliminate the prejudices inferred by price, name and region.

claret A uniquely Anglo-Saxon term, originating from the Middle Ages, for the red wines of Bordeaux. At the time, red and white grapes were grown alongside each other in the vineyard and vinified together, producing a lighter-coloured red than is the norm today. The French called it *clairet*, meaning light red.

disgorgement The part of the traditional sparkling winemaking process that expels sediment (the residue of a second fermentation) from the neck of the bottle. Invented by the Veuve (Widow) Clicquot in 1816, manual disgorgement inevitably wasted a quantity of Champagne. The long foil on the neck of a bottle was to hide the fact that it was not full. Modern disgorgement involves freezing the neck in order to expel only the frozen sediment prior to the bottle being topped up.

***méthode champenoise* (Champagne method)** A term which uniquely describes the intricate process of making Champagne. Integral to the Champagne method is that the wine is grown, made and bottled in the Champagne region of France. A landmark European legal case in 1994 ruled that no other region can use the term. Therefore, sparkling wines made in the same way elsewhere in France or Europe are commonly described as *méthode traditionelle* (traditional method).

remuage The French word for riddling, which is part of the Champagne-making process. Racked bottles are periodically agitated by hand or by machines known as gyro-pallettes in order to gather lees from the second fermentation in the neck of the sealed bottle ready for disgorgement.

Premier Cru, Grand Cru The quality classifications enshrined in the French Appellation (AOC) systems, but whose significance varies from region to region. *Cru* translates as 'growth' and can refer to a single vineyard or group of vineyards. On Bordeaux's 'Left Bank', only the five top wines are Premiers Crus Classés (First Growths). In St-Emilion, on the Right Bank, the top 13 wines are known as Premiers Grands Crus Classés and some 64 Grands Crus Classés estates ranked below them. In Burgundy and Champagne, Grand Cru ('Great Growth') is the top-quality classification, followed by Premier Cru. Alsace has no Premier Cru classification but around 13 per cent of its vineyards are classified Grands Crus.

rootstock The root of the vine on to which canes are grafted to produce fruit-bearing plants. Most rootstocks used today come from phylloxera-resistant, native American vine species or hybrids. *Vitis vinifera* is particularly susceptible to attack from the phylloxera louse. The most resistant American vine species are *Vitis riparia, V. rupestris* and *V. berlandieri*.

varietal A wine made entirely (or almost entirely, depending on local wine laws) from a single grape variety. The concept was pioneered in California as early as the 1950s and 1960s but really gained traction in the 1970s when Napa Valley winemakers such as Robert Mondavi began marketing Cabernet Sauvignon and Chardonnay. Varietal wines soon became the norm in other New World countries, especially Australia, New Zealand and South Africa. A varietal wine is distinct from one named after its region of origin (or inspiration) such as Chablis, Burgundy and Champagne.

WINE'S SPIRITUAL BEGINNINGS

the 30-second wine

Wine began as a spiritual, not a secular, good, and for much of its history was consumed as a way of communing with the divine.

3-MINUTE TOP-UP
The ancients may have regarded wine as heavenly alchemy, but by all accounts it did not taste heavenly. When exposed to too much air, all wine turns sour. To disguise its vinegariness, winemakers added myriad flavourings – herbs, spices, honey, marble dust, myrrh and, most notably, pine resin. The most valued wines were invariably those with the most flavourings. Thick and oily, they tasted more syrupy than sublime.

Throughout most of its

8,000-year history wine was not prized primarily as a source of pleasure or even sustenance but rather as a means of communion with one's god or gods. Fermentation, being a natural process, meant that the transformation of fresh grape juice into alcoholic wine could occur without human hand, making the drink seem magical, mysterious – surely divine intervention? And since wine made people feel good, it seemed to promise connection to a supernatural or transcendent realm. In ancient cultures, from Neolithic Transcaucasia (where wine was first drunk regularly) to Anatolia, the Levant, Egypt, Greece and Rome, wine was deemed to be a gift from the gods. It was at heart spiritual, and imbibing offered a way to literally sense the divine nature of creation. Especially in classical Greece and then in Rome, where wine-drinking became commonplace, the heady beverage also provided indulgence – sometimes debauched – for the rich, and nourishment for the poor. But until the rise of a religion that distinguished sharply between secular and sacred, wine never lost its spiritual essence. For early Christians, communion wine – the Blood of God – was very different from the drink that slaked thirst or quickened passion. In previous cultures, however, all wine was equal: heavenly because god-like.

RELATED TOPICS
See also
FERMENTATION
page 32

MEDIEVAL MONKS
page 82

3-SECOND BIOGRAPHIES
DIONYSUS
Greek wine god who lived on in ancient Rome under the name Bacchus

EURIPIDES
c. 480–406 BCE
Greek tragedian whose *Bacchae* depicts Dionysus as inhabiting the wine itself

PLINY THE ELDER
23–79 CE
Roman author whose *Natural History* provides a detailed record of early wine culture

30-SECOND TEXT
Paul Lukacs

Wine has been revered, blessed and enjoyed throughout the ages by rulers, popes and ordinary people.

MEDIEVAL MONKS

the 30-second wine

3-SECOND SIP
Cistercian monks in Burgundy during the twelfth and the thirteenth centuries were the first people to realize the full significance of place in a wine's identity.

3-MINUTE TOP-UP
The most famous Cistercian wine of all came from the Clos de Vougeot, a walled vineyard in Burgundy that the monks tended for six centuries and that today is owned by over 80 separate growers. An English visitor near the end of the order's ownership remarked in awe that the places they had chosen reveal the 'righteous attention they give to things of the spirit'.

A small fraternity of white-habited monks made the most celebrated wines in Europe during the Middle Ages. They discovered what centuries later came to be called terroir, the magical ability of a particular place to impart an identifiable character to the wines made from grapes grown there. These monks belonged to the Cistercian order, an exceptionally devout society that shunned worldly wealth but embraced manual labour. Starting in Burgundy, they recorded in meticulous detail which vineyard plots produced the healthiest crops. Only a few paces could separate an excellent site from an ordinary one, and the monks constructed stone walls around the best, designating each one as a *clos* – a cloistered, enclosed place. The wines from those places tasted special because different, and different because particular. They became the favourites of kings and queens, dukes and bishops – and even popes. Before long, lay farmers adopted similar practices in their own vineyards, and the new focus on place expanded to include parts of Alsace, the Loire and Rhône valleys, and the hillsides along both the rivers Mosel and Rhine in Germany. By literally rooting the character of their wines in the singularity of place, the Cistercian monks had given wine something it never had before – individuality.

RELATED TOPICS
See also
TERROIR
page 16

BURGUNDY
page 102

3-SECOND BIOGRAPHIES
BERNARD DE CLARVAUX
1090–1153
French abbot and the founder of the Cistercian order

POPE URBAN V
1310–70
Provençal Benedictine who refused to move to Rome in part because he loved the new Burgundy wines

30-SECOND TEXT
Paul Lukacs

Monks assumed the habit of winemaking established by the ancients, developing vital techniques and identifying many of the finest vineyards in Europe.

BORDEAUX'S RISE TO PROMINENCE
the 30-second wine

RELATED TOPICS
See also
CABERNET SAUVIGNON
& CHÂTEAU LATOUR
page 62

WHY CHAMPAGNE SPARKLES
page 86

BORDEAUX
page 100

3-SECOND SIP
A new sort of red Bordeaux wine, tasting unlike any made before, emerged in the mid-seventeenth century and by 1800 had become the most prestigious wine in the entire world.

3-MINUTE TOP-UP
During the first half of the nineteenth century, various people tried to organize or rank the wide range of red Bordeaux wines coming on to the market every year. In 1855 an official committee issued a report in which they classified the region's top wines, the first growths being those that consistently fetched the highest prices. That report, known as the Bordeaux 1855 classifcation, still holds sway today.

'A good and most particular taste' is how the English diarist Samuel Pepys described his first experience with the new red wines coming from Bordeaux in the seventeenth and eighteenth centuries. Wine had been made in the marshy lowlands between the rivers Garonne and Dordogne since the Romans first occupied the region. During the Middle Ages, *clairet*, a pinkish blend, became popular in northern Europe, where trade in it made many fortunes. Like most medieval wines, however, it tasted generic rather than particular, and so was a far cry from the dark red that Pepys admired. The new breed of red Bordeaux, led by those from an estate called Haut-Brion, displayed distinctive flavours and aromas. Sometimes called 'clarets', they tasted special because they were particular. Their particularity came in part from the grapes being grown in gravelly, well-drained sites, which encouraged even and relatively rapid ripening, and in part from the meticulous attention that ambitious vintners gave them. Before long, Haut-Brion was joined by other estates that remain famous today. With names like Lafite, Latour and Margaux, these became by 1800 the most revered wines in the world. Not only did they taste good, but drinking them signalled that one had good taste.

3-SECOND BIOGRAPHIES
ARNAUD III DE PONTAC
1599–1681
French owner of Haut-Brion who led the way in creating a new style of Bordeaux wine

SAMUEL PEPYS
1633–1703
English diarist who penned the first tasting note on the new Bordeaux wines

30-SECOND TEXT
Paul Lukacs

Bordeaux's wines were famous by the Middle Ages but it was the 1855 classification under Napoleon III that confirmed its status.

GRANDS VINS DE BORDEAUX

Maison fondée

MARGAUX

Mis en bouteille dans nos chais

HAUT-BRION

WHY CHAMPAGNE SPARKLES

the 30-second wine

3-SECOND SIP
Making Champagne
sparkle became possible
following a series of
discoveries, starting with
the invention of strong
glass that allowed wine to
continue to ferment in the
bottle, trapping its bubbles
until the cork is popped.

3-MINUTE TOP-UP
Contrary to legend, French
Benedictine monk Dom
Pérignon did not invent
bubbly Champagne. No
single individual did. Dom
Pérignon, however, was
a master blender. While
he made still wines, his
insistence on using the right
grape varieties in the right
proportions was copied by
other vintners, including
clerics, much later when
Champagne finally began
to sparkle.

Though grapes had long been cultivated in Champagne in northern France, sparkling wine was invented there over a span of two centuries, beginning in the late 1600s. Fermentation converts sugar into alcohol and carbon dioxide, causing all wines to effervesce; Champagne was created when winemakers were able to trap the bubbles inside the bottle. The first step was the development of sturdy glass bottles and secure stoppers. The second followed the discovery that adding sugar could make the region's tart wines taste richer. The difficulty, however, was knowing how much sugar: too little produced too few bubbles; too much exerted pressure that would break the bottle. But in 1838 a professor invented an instrument to measure the sugar and accurately predict the resultant pressure. Two decades earlier, Champagne Clicquot Ponsardin's cellarmaster had devised a method of inverting and twisting Champagne bottles – riddling – in order to remove the yeasty sediment. Then a Belgian inventor developed a process of freezing the neck of the bottle to expel the spent yeast but save the sparkle. Together, these innovations resulted in a wine that exploded in popularity. In 1800, Champagne was producing about 300,000 bottles of frothy wine. A century later, the figure was 30 million; today it is over 300 million.

RELATED TOPICS
See also
FERMENTATION
page 32

MAKING CHAMPAGNE
page 40

CLOSURES
page 48

3-SECOND BIOGRAPHIES
DOM PIERRE PÉRIGNON
1638–1715
French treasurer of the Abbey
of Hautvillers in Champagne,
who popularized sparkling wines
from that region

ANDRÉ FRANÇOIS
fl. 1836
French professor who invented
an instrument for measuring
sugar and pressure in sparkling
wine

30-SECOND TEXT
Paul Lukacs

Champagne is not the only wine to sparkle but it has the reputation for being the best, owing to its climate, geology and production method.

A CENTURY OF CRISES

the 30-second wine

Wine bathed briefly in glory in

the nineteenth century. Increased affluence among Europe's expanding middle class brought wines, previously imbibed only by the rich, to a wider public, eager to express their good taste. Beginning in the 1850s, however, wine endured a series of crises. Some were agricultural, others cultural; collectively they caused wine to plummet in prestige. First came disease – mildews, black rot and phylloxera, all brought to Europe on American vines. Sprays to combat mildews were developed and over 99 per cent of the continent's vineyards had to be replanted with resistant rootstocks in response to phylloxera – a process that took nearly two generations for growers to recover. Meanwhile, poor-quality imported wine, much from North Africa and much sold under false labels, flooded the market. Fine wine's reputation was damaged, and drinkers sought an alternative with which to make merry. They found it first in absinthe and other harsh distillates, then in cocktails. Increasingly winemakers felt under siege; some literally had been in 1914 and would be again in 1939, when war impoverished markets and bombs exploded in vineyards. Shaken, not stirred, wine's fortunes ultimately recovered spectacularly in the second half of the twentieth century.

RELATED TOPICS
See also
PHYLLOXERA
page 24

3-SECOND BIOGRAPHY
JOSEPHINE BAKER
1906–75
American-born dancer and singer whose erotic performances shocked the beau monde; also a cocktail named in her honour

30-SECOND TEXT
Paul Lukacs

3-SECOND SIP
Calamity followed calamity for a full century, challenging wine's status as a drink of refined choice in many people's minds.

3-MINUTE TOP-UP
Some classic cocktails included wine, among them the Kir (white wine and crème de cassis), the Bellini (Prosecco and white peach purée) and the Champagne Cocktail (Champagne, sugar and bitters). Paradoxically, though, because these drinks relied more on the bartender's than the vintner's skill, they further contributed to wine's decline in esteem.

In 1920s America, Prohibition and 'dry' crusaders meant spirits of dubious provenance were disguised with powerfully flavoured mixers and concoctions such as the Martini, Sidecar and Gin Fizz became all the rage.

THE START OF APPELLATIONS

the 30-second wine

3-SECOND SIP
AOC is France's certification of a wine's quality and a guarantee of its provenance, a system that is also used to classify produce as diverse as cheese and chickens, lentils and lavender.

3-MINUTE TOP-UP
The first AOC rules were formulated by Pierre Le Roy de Boiseaumarié in 1923 in Châteauneuf-du-Pape in the southern Rhône Valley. He drew the appellation's borders, set minimum alcohol levels and limited both yields and the varieties permitted. Châteauneuf, previously a source of mostly cheap bulk wines, produces some of France's most prestigious ones.

Wine's return to popularity and prestige after a century of crises began with a return to its roots, literally, with renewed focus on terroir, the unique particularities of 'place'. A crucial first step was the creation of appellations in France in the 1920s. Individual geographical units were designated as appellations to guarantee the authenticity of any wine made with grapes grown there. Regulations mandated not only where the wine came from but also which varieties went into it and how it had to be made. While keeping some existing practices, others were discarded and new ones were added, compelling vintners who wanted to use appellation names to improve quality. No longer could red Burgundy include cheap wine from southern France, or Bordeaux have barrels of Spanish red in the blend. Everything was legislated, from size of crop to how long the wine was aged. As the initial *Appellation d'origine contrôlée* (controlled designation of origin) or AOC rules decreed, winemakers had to follow 'loyal, local and constant' practices. Similar legislation and appellation systems were instituted in other wine-producing countries during the second half of the century. Though not always as restrictive, they had the cumulative effect of raising quality worldwide and making the label on a wine bottle something that consumers could again trust.

RELATED TOPICS
See also
TERROIR
page 16

MEDIEVAL MONKS
page 82

A CENTURY OF CRISES
page 88

3-SECOND BIOGRAPHIES
JOSEPH CAPUS
1867–1947
French legislator who spearheaded the movement to create controlled appellations throughout France

PIERRE LE ROY DE BOISEAUMARIÉ
1890–1967
French wine estate owner who created France's first official appellation

30-SECOND TEXT
Paul Lukacs

France's appellation system for quality wines can designate a single vineyard in Burgundy or an entire valley such as the Loire.

THE JUDGMENT OF PARIS

the 30-second wine

In May 1976, Steven Spurrier, an Englishman with a wine shop in Paris, organized a wine tasting at the Paris Intercontinental Hotel. Nine eminent French wine professionals gathered to taste and evaluate 20 wines – red Bordeaux, white Burgundies and some Cabernet Sauvignons and Chardonnays from north California. None expected the American wines to perform well and the results of the blind tasting shocked everyone. When all 20 wines had been swirled, savoured and spat out, the highest-ranking wine in each category was from Napa Valley; Chardonnay Chateau Montelena 1973 in the whites section and Cabernet Sauvignon Stag's Leap Wine Cellar 1973 in the reds section. Suddenly California, and by extension all New World wine regions, had to be taken seriously as sources of truly fine wine. Over the next two decades, similar tastings featured wines from Argentina, Australia, Chile, New Zealand, South Africa and more. While non-European wines did not always win, they continually demonstrated their place in such august company. Modern science in vineyards and wineries, coupled with an investment, had resulted in ever-more excellent wines coming from ever-more places. By the start of the twenty-first century, the fine-wine map, once confined to western Europe, had become truly global.

RELATED TOPICS
See also
TERROIR
page 16

NAPA VALLEY
page 106

3-SECOND SIP
The 1976 Paris tasting heralded the emergence of new wines from new places that could compete with Europe's best.

3-MINUTE TOP-UP
The judges at the Paris tasting confused the different wines, ascribing to the Californians attributes like delicacy and finesse that they assumed had to be French. At that time, such confusion was the highest compliment one could pay a New World wine. More recently, however, New World vintners have stopped labouring to imitate foreign models and begun to allow their own wines to assert an identity coming from their native terroir.

3-SECOND BIOGRAPHIES
WARREN WINIARSKI
1928–
Californian owner and winemaker at Stag's Leap Wine Cellars, whose Cabernet Sauvignon triumphed in Paris

STEVEN SPURRIER
1941–
British wine merchant who organized the 1976 tasting that would become historic

PIERRE BRÉJOUX
French head of the Institut National des Appellations d'Origine, and chief judge at the Paris tasting

30-SECOND TEXT
Paul Lukacs

Careers were made and expectations confounded when California's wines triumphed over France's in the 1976 blind tasting.

18 June 1913
Born in Virginia,
Minnesota

1937
Graduates in economics
from Stanford University
and later begins work at
the Sunnyhill winery
St Helena

1943
Cesare Mondavi acquires
the Charles Krug Winery
in St Helena with sons
Robert and Peter

1966
Establishes the Robert
Mondavi Winery with his
two sons on the Oakville
Highway, Napa Valley

1968
Markets the first
Fumé-Blanc, a dry,
oak-aged Sauvignon.
The style (and name)
was so successful it was
widely copied, as far
afield as Australia

1968
Releases his first
Cabernet Sauvignon,
a milestone in the
Napa Valley's modern
renaissance

1979
Establishes the Mondavi
Woodbridge Winery in
Lodi, California to focus
on higher volume,
lower-priced wines

1985
Introduces high-
density plantings of
Cabernet Sauvignon
vines to reduce yields
and maximize fruit
concentration

1989
Selected as *Decanter*
Man of the Year

1995
Creates a joint venture
with Tuscany's Marchesi
de Frescobaldi,
producing several labels
including Luce and
Lucente

2002
Receives the Order of
Merit of the Italian
Republic

2005
Receives the Legion of
Honour from the French
government

2007
Inducted into the
California Hall of Fame

16 May 2008
Dies just short of his
95th birthday

2008
University of California,
Davis opens The Robert
Mondavi Institute for
Wine and Food Science.
Mondavi had helped
fund it to the tune of
$25 million

ROBERT MONDAVI

Winemaker and philanthropist,
Robert Mondavi was among the most significant
figures in post-Prohibition California wine. He
helped take an industry from the doldrums to one
that could compete confidently on the world stage.
For almost five decades he inspired a generation
of ambitious winemakers and introduced millions
of consumers to modern California wine.

Mondavi's big break came in 1943 when his
parents bought the Charles Krug Winery in St
Helena. Working here with his bother Peter, he
refined his knowledge of winemaking through
experimentation and guidance from famous
oenologist André Tchelistcheff.

During the 1950s Mondavi became increasingly
focused on the Cabernet Sauvignon grape which
led him, in 1962, to Bordeaux. The trip heightened
his appreciation of fine wine, fine food and
culture, related themes which were to feature
throughout his later life.

After a bitter dispute with his brother in 1965,
he left the family business and with his two sons,
established the Napa Valley's first major new
winery for decades. It soon became one of the
most successful in the USA. The architecturally
imposing, 'Mission-style' Robert Mondavi Winery
was in the vanguard of technical and marketing
innovation, introducing temperature-controlled
fermentation and championing the use of French
oak barrels. Mondavi also popularized the now
common practice of selling wine by grape variety.

His unerring belief in Napa's world-class
potential was vindicated in 1976 when local wines
out-performed top ranking Bordeaux and Burgundy
in the landmark tasting known as the Judgment
of Paris. The winning wines were made by Mike
Grgich, winemaker at Chateau Montelena and
Warren Winiarski, owner-winemaker of Stag's
Leap Wine Cellar, both of whom had previously
worked for Mondavi.

Mondavi's long-held ambition to create an
ultra-premium wine came to fruition in 1979 after
years of discussion with Bordeaux luminary Baron
Philippe de Rothschild. The Opus One joint venture
between their two families was formally announced
in 1980. Its success inspired further Mondavi
partnerships in Chile with the Chadwick family,
and in Tuscany with the Marchesi de Frescobaldi.

From the 1970s, the Mondavi Winery also
drove Napa Valley's bourgeoning cultural scene,
hosting glamorous events from international
culinary seminars to an acclaimed annual Summer
Music Festival.

Active well into his late eighties, Robert
Mondavi was also prominent in the fight
against America's anti-alcohol lobby. An iconic
wine patriarch whose legacy lives on, he was
posthumously inducted into the California Hall of
Fame in 2007 by Governor Arnold Schwarzenegger
and First Lady Maria Shriver.

ICONIC REGIONS

ICONIC REGIONS
GLOSSARY

1855 Classification A hierarchy of Bordeaux best wine estates drawn up for the Paris Exhibition of 1855. It covered the red wines of the Médoc and the sweet wines of Sauternes-Barsac and was based upon average market prices over many decades. The one geographical exception was the famous Château Haut-Brion, a Premier Cru Classé (First Growth) in the Graves region. The classification has remained intact for over 150 years, although in 1973 Baron Philippe de Rothschild of Château Mouton-Rothschild was successful in lobbying for his estate to be elevated to First Growth status.

carbonic maceration A method of making red wine starting with whole, uncrushed bunches of grapes. A non-yeast-driven fermentation begins inside each berry in an anaerobic environment converting sugars to alcohol. Carbon dioxide, a byproduct of fermentation, eventually causes the grapes to burst, allowing fermentation to continue in the normal aerobic manner. This is the principle behind winemaking in Beaujolais and results in an overtly fruity and supple wine.

claret A uniquely Anglo-Saxon term, originating from the Middle Ages, for the red wines of Bordeaux. At the time, red and white grapes were vinified together, producing a lighter-coloured red than is the norm today. The French called it *clairet*, meaning light red.

climat A French term for a specific, often very small, area of a vineyard with its own distinct terroir. It may be known by its historic name or *lieu-dit*. In Burgundy, *climat* is used as a synonym for vineyard. If it has its own appellation and is wholly owned by a single grower it is called a monopole.

Côte d'Or A French *département*, and the heart of the Burgundy wine region comprising the Côte de Beaune and the Côte de Nuits. Its capital is Beaune.

domaine A French word for a wine-growing estate, especially in Burgundy but also used in other regions of France. In Bordeaux the more common term for a wine estate is château, which may or may not have a grand residence at its centre.

Échelle des Crus A system developed in Champagne in the mid-twentieth century to distinguish the quality of grapes grown in different villages and to set prices accordingly (échelle means 'ladder'). Villages rated 90–99 per cent are Premiers Crus while 100 per cent-rated villages are Grands Crus. Originally, growers received the corresponding percentage of the declared grapes' price. Today pricing is more flexible.

First Growths The elite group of five châteaux in the Médoc and Graves regions of Bordeaux ranked Premiers Crus in the 1855 Classification. They are Châteaux Latour, Lafite-Rothschild, Mouton-Rothschild, Margaux and Haut-Brion.

international varieties Grape varieties that stem from the classic wine regions of Europe and are today grown through the wine-producing world. The top varieties are sometimes referred to as the noble grapes. Of the reds these are Cabernet Sauvignon, Merlot, Pinot Noir and Syrah/Shiraz. Of the whites, Riesling, Chardonnay, Semillon, Sauvignon Blanc and Chenin Blanc.

The Médoc The best-known wine district of Bordeaux that extends north of the city and west of the Gironde estuary. It is often referred to as Bordeaux's 'Left Bank' and most famously encompasses eight appellations including the Haut-Médoc communes of Margaux, St-Julien, Pauillac and St-Estèphe. It was the subject of the 1855 Classification, still in use today.

Monopole see *Climat*

Premier Cru, Grand Cru The vineyard quality classifications enshrined in French Appellation (AOC) systems, but whose significance varies from region to region. The word *cru* translates as 'growth' and can refer to a single vineyard or group of vineyards. On Bordeaux's 'Left Bank', the five top wines are called Premiers Crus Classés or First Growths. In St-Emilion, on the Right Bank, the top 13 wines are known as Premiers Grands Crus Classés and some 64 Grands Crus Classés estates ranked below them.In Burgundy and Champagne, Grand Cru (or 'Great Growth') is the top-quality classification followed by Premier Cru. Alsace has no Premier Cru classification but around 13 per cent of its vineyards are classified Grands Crus.

varietal A wine made entirely (or almost entirely, depending on local wine laws) from a single grape variety. The concept was pioneered in California as early as the 1950s but really gained traction in the 1970s when Napa Valley winemakers such as Robert Mondavi began marketing Cabernet Sauvignon and Chardonnay. Varietal wines soon became the norm in other New World countries, especially Australia, New Zealand and South Africa. A varietal wine is distinct from one named after its region of origin such as Chablis, Burgundy and Champagne.

BORDEAUX
the 30-second wine

RELATED TOPICS
See also
SWEET WINES
page 42

CABERNET SAUVIGNON
& CHÂTEAU LATOUR
page 62

BORDEAUX'S RISE TO
PROMINENCE
page 84

A CENTURY OF CRISES
page 88

THE START OF APPELLATIONS
page 90

3-SECOND SIP
Bordeaux has a
long-established reputation
as the home of some of
the most expensive red
and sweet white wines
in the world.

3-MINUTE TOP-UP
The 1855 Médoc
Classification is Bordeaux's
most famous quality
hierarchy. It ranks the
estates (châteaux) rather
than the quality of
vineyards and has five
levels, classed as 'growths'.
First Growth châteaux
are those at the pinnacle
and usually command the
highest prices. There are
five First Growth properties:
Mouton-Rothschild, Latour,
Lafite-Rothschild, Margaux
and Haut-Brion, the last of
which was upgraded (which
seldom happens) in 1973/74.

Bordeaux is arguably the most
famous wine region in the world, located close
to the city with the same name on the south-west
coast of France. All red Bordeaux wines are given
the moniker 'claret', and although much everyday
claret is made, it is the upper echelons that take
the lion's share of attention – whether it's the
painstaking analysis over weather conditions each
year, its performance as an investment wine or the
influence of American critic Robert Parker on prices.
Claret is often defined as whether it is 'Left Bank'
or 'Right Bank'. Although almost never the sole
grape of the blend, Cabernet Sauvignon thrives
on the gravelly soils of two Left Bank locations;
the Médoc, which is north of Bordeaux city, and
Graves, south of the city and west of the river
Garonne. On the Right Bank, east of the river
Dordogne, the heavier clay soils are more suitable
for Merlot, often blended with Cabernet Franc.
Malbec and Petit Verdot are less popular grapes
but can form part of the blends of some red
Bordeaux. Dry white Bordeaux is typically a blend
of Sauvignon Blanc and Semillon, which, together
with Muscadelle, are the varieties used to make
Bordeaux's famous sweet wines, in subregions
such as Sauternes and Barsac.

30-SECOND TEXT
Jane Parkinson

*Bordeaux's châteaux
are dedicated to
making fine wines.
Red, Cabernet blends
dominate production
but white wines
likewise range from
good to sublime.*

Château
Mouton Rothschild

BURGUNDY

the 30-second wine

Burgundy, the limestone ridge

running almost exactly north-south in north-east France is often placed on a pedestal for making benchmark Pinot Noir and Chardonnay, its protagonist varieties. Its most sought-after wines come from the Côte d'Or, which itself is divided in two: Côte de Nuits, where Pinot Noir strongly dominates, and Côte de Beaune, which is more (though not exclusively) Chardonnay territory. Most Burgundy producers are referred to as 'domaines', including the most famous property: Domaine de la Romanée-Conti, which makes the most rarified and costly Pinot Noir in the world. Anecdotally, the subregions north and south of the Côte d'Or are at times excluded from being labelled 'Burgundy': Chablis in the cooler north is the name of the region, the town and its brisk and racy dry white wine, made purely from Chardonnay. To the south are the Côte Chalonnaise and the Mâconnais, which make recognizably Burgundian red and white wines as well as a softly sparkling version – *crémant de Bourgogne*. Further south, Beaujolais (unlike Chablis) is officially outside the appellation; its style of wine is entirely different from 'red Burgundy' because it is made from the Gamay grape, and often undergoes a process called carbonic maceration, which lends Beaujolais a distinctive fruity character.

3-SECOND SIP
Red Burgundy and white Burgundy from the Côte d'Or are widely regarded as the ultimate manifestation of Pinot Noir and Chardonnay, respectively.

3-MINUTE TOP-UP
The Napoleonic laws of inheritance, under which land must be shared equally among a deceased person's children, have greatly contributed to the Burgundian landscape. Today, a complicated patchwork of vineyards exists, leaving growers to tend minute plots. This explains why famous vineyard names, with their own appellation such as Le Montrachet or Le Chambertin, can be used by several producers.

RELATED TOPICS
See also
PINOT NOIR &
LA ROMANÉE-CONTI
page 64

MEDIEVAL MONKS
page 82

30-SECOND TEXT
Jane Parkinson

Burgundy is a landscape of small parcels of vines that yield some of the most superlative expressions of Pinot Noir and Chardonnay made anywhere on Earth.

1984

TUSCANY

the 30-second wine

This celebrated region in central Italy champions one grape above all others for red wine: Sangiovese, the main component of Chianti, Tuscany's most famous wine region. Chianti has two key areas: Chianti Classico, the heart of the region and considered its best part, and Chianti, which is itself divided into seven subregions, all of which can produce enjoyable wines, especially those from the Rufina subregion. On the slopes around the hill-town of Montalcino, where temperatures are hotter than in Chianti, Brunello makes one of Tuscany's signature wines. Intense, tannic and bold, Brunello di Montalcino usually needs a good decade to soften for optimum drinking. Its earlier-maturing sibling Rosso di Montalcino has courted controversy in recent years (which is now resolved), owing to confusion over the grapes included in its blend. Tuscany also makes sweet and dry white wines. Richly flavoured Vin Santo is usually made from Trebbiano and Malvasia grapes laid on straw or hung up to air-dry in order to concentrate the sugars. Tuscany's best dry white wines come from the coast, where the Vermentino grape makes zesty and refreshing whites to quench local thirst.

RELATED TOPICS
See also
SWEET WINES
page 42

30-SECOND TEXT
Jane Parkinson

3-SECOND SIP
Savoury, tannic and tasting of cherries, Sangiovese is Tuscany's best indigenous red-wine variety.

3-MINUTE TOP-UP
Tuscany's most revered and notorious wines are those that broke Italian wine rules back in the 1970s. Producers of expensive wines from non-native grapes such as Cabernet Sauvignon and Merlot had to market them as 'declassified' because use of such grapes prohibited them from being included in Italy's wine quality hierarchy until 1992 when a new designation, IGT (*Indicazione Geografica Tipica*), was created for this superlative class of wines. The 'Super Tuscans' now rank among the most sought-after wines in the world. Famous – and memorable – names include Ornellaia, Masseto, Sassicaia and Tignaello.

Italy is blessed with ideal conditions for growing grapes, and, lying at its heart, is Tuscany whose ancient winemaking pedigree rested on local grapes. Planting international varieties alongside the all-Italian classics has resulted in some remarkable wines.

NAPA VALLEY

the 30-second wine

If wine regions were royalty,

Napa Valley would be reigning monarch in California and indeed the USA. Situated 112 kilometres (70 miles) north of San Francisco, Napa's first winery was founded in the second half of the nineteenth century and many followed suit. However, phylloxera and then Prohibition halted its ambitions. In 1966, Robert Mondavi, widely regarded as the region's founding father, opened his winery, swiftly followed by others. Napa staked its place in wine history in 1976 at the so-called Judgment of Paris, a blind tasting held in Paris, when two Napa wines – one white, one red – triumphed over famous French wines in their respective categories. Since then the region has been transformed into a sophisticated tourist-friendly wine hub. Cabernet Sauvignon is Napa's most cherished and admired grape, especially in the American Viticultural Areas (AVA) of Oakville and Rutherford, where the wines are robust and powerful, the best capable of ageing for decades. Red grapes Merlot and Zinfandel are also grown and Pinot Noir is favoured in the south, while Chardonnay is easily the most significant white grape. Napa is also home to several of California's 'cult' wines such as Screaming Eagle, Harlan, Araujo, Colgin Cellars, Dalla Valle and Grace Family.

RELATED TOPICS
See also
CABERNET SAUVIGNON
& CHÂTEAU LATOUR
page 62

REGIONAL GRAPES
& WINE STYLES
page 74

THE JUDGMENT OF PARIS
page 92

30-SECOND TEXT
Jane Parkinson

3-SECOND SIP
Napa Valley is the USA's most prestigious wine region, especially renowned for its intense Cabernet Sauvignon wines.

3-MINUTE TOP-UP
Set between the Vaca and Mayacamas mountain ranges, Napa experiences great temperature variation, which accounts for significant differences in grape plantings and wine styles along its 50 kilometre (30-mile) strip. Calistoga, its most northerly point, makes Cabernet Sauvignon that is rich and meaty. Here the average summer temperature is several degrees higher than in Los Carneros down south, which explains why Pinot Noir is Carneros' grape of choice for still and sparkling wines with an enviable reputation.

Once seen as a remote fruit-farming district, Napa Valley is now the symbol as well as the heart of California's top-quality wine production.

RIOJA

the 30-second wine

South of Bilbao, Rioja is the

region of northern-central Spain that until recently was considered the exclusive source of the country's best red wines; today it shares that reputation with Ribera del Duero and Priorat. Rioja straddles the river Ebro as it heads south-east from Haro, spanning an area so vast it is subdivided into three zones: Rioja Alta, Rioja Alavesa and Rioja Baja. Rioja follows a hierarchy that stipulates minimum ageing periods of the wine both in barrel and bottle. The higher the quality of the wine, the longer it is aged. In descending order this ranking runs Gran Reserva, Reserva, Crianza and Rioja, although a new wave of quality producers has tended to disregard that classification. Tempranillo is the chief grape used in red Rioja, although as a style that is typically blended, Garnacha is also of huge importance. Graciano and Mazuelo (Carignan) are common components of red Rioja, albeit to a lesser extent, while Cabernet Sauvignon has also taken root here. Red Rioja's most famous producer is Marqués de Murrieta Castillo Ygay. White Rioja is often – and unfairly – overlooked: it is usually made from a blend of local white grapes: Viura, Malvasia Riojana and/or Garnacha Blanca.

RELATED TOPICS
See also
MAKING RED WINE
page 38

ÉLEVAGE
page 46

TEMPRANILLO &
RIBERA DEL DUERO
page 70

30-SECOND TEXT
Jane Parkinson

3-SECOND SIP
A name that is familiar and appreciated around the world, Rioja is a Spanish region of considerable reputation making everything from everyday wines to some of the country's most prized.

3-MINUTE TOP-UP
The style of red Rioja has been a constant source of debate and discussion. Historically red Rioja was made using American oak barrels, imparting a telltale vanilla character to the wine. In the last 20 years winemaking has been tweaked and French oak became popular, producing 'modern Rioja', which is fruitier and darker than traditional red Rioja. Today, as producers try to re-authenticate red Rioja, American barrels are back in favour.

To outsiders red Rioja once was the Spanish wine: full-bodied, light-hued and heavily oaked, which gives a marked vanilla flavour. These days the blend is smoother, fruitier and more delicately oaked.

VINOS FINOS
de
RIOJA
Denominación de Origen Calificada
2006

Embotellado por

R. Lopez de Heredia Viña Tondonia

75 Cl.   13% VOL
RE.SELLO VIÑEDOS Y BODEGAS EN
HARO·RIOJA ALTA·ESPAÑA
PRODUCTO DE ESPAÑA

F U N D A D A   E N   18

VIÑA
CUBILLO

75 cl.   12,5%vol

GRAN RESERVA
1982

MURIEL
RIOJA
DENOMINACION DE ORIGEN CALIFICADA
Embotellado por
BODEGAS MURIEL, S.A.
Elciego (Rioja Alavesa) España
PRODUCT OF SPAIN

STELLENBOSCH

the 30-second wine

The traditional hub of South

Africa's best-quality wines, Stellenbosch, is 45 kilometres (28 miles) east of Cape Town. The district is steeped in history and renowned for its characteristic settler architecture – white-painted Cape Dutch buildings dot a landscape blanketed with vineyards. The best Stellenbosch wines are often said to come from regions closest to the quaint university town of the same name, where cooling coastal breezes off False Bay delay ripening, generating a desirable lengthier process of maturation for the grapes. Stellenbosch favours the production of red over white wine these days, although excellent white wines are produced, especially from the vines on soils (which vary greatly inthe region) that are lighter and sandier, and are chiefly made using Chenin Blanc, Sauvignon Blanc or Chardonnay. Red Stellenbosch wines are made as varietals or blends – often called Cape Blends. Red grapes that prosper include Cabernet Sauvignon, Shiraz, Merlot and Pinotage (a variety distinctive to South Africa, created in Stellenbosch University, partly in response to the deadly phylloxera that took hold here at the turn of the twentieth century). Several of South Africa's most revered wine estates are based in Stellenbosch including Vergelegen, Meerlust, Jordan, Warwick, Simonsberg and Neil Ellis.

RELATED TOPICS
See also
PHYLLOXERA
page 24

REGIONAL GRAPES & WINE STYLES
page 74

30-SECOND TEXT
Jane Parkinson

International varieties including Cabernet Sauvignon, Merlot, Chenin Blanc and Chardonnay feature prominently in blends from Stellenbosch. This region is also famous for Pinotage (a cross between Pinot Noir and Cinsaut), a grape that is unique to South Africa that makes typically dark- hued wine with pronounced berry and liquorice flavours.

ANNO 1796

MARLBOROUGH

the 30-second wine

Located on the north-eastern tip

of South Island, Marlborough is New Zealand's biggest wine region. Its name in Maori means 'the place with the hole in the cloud', in reference to the intense sunshine. Sauvignon Blanc rules here: although Montana was the first winery to commercially plant the grape its success is largely attributed to one producer, Cloudy Bay, which released an exotic-tasting Sauvignon with an evocative label back in the 1980s. The style was not difficult to replicate, and soon a sea of Marlborough Sauvignon Blanc that tasted of liquid passion fruit was made, and remains in huge demand today. If Marlborough's economy has thrived on making this style of wine, its relationship with Sauvignon Blanc is a source of pride and increasing frustration, as Marlborough strives to prove it isn't merely a one-trick pony. This has manifested itself variously, from putting Sauvignon Blanc in oak barrels, producing a longer-lived, food-friendlier style, to making high-class Chardonnay. Today, vineyard capacity is close to its limit, owing to lack of land and tighter control over water rights, while sustainable winemaking is a key initiative for the whole industry.

RELATED TOPICS
See also
MAKING WHITE WINE
page 36

ÉLEVAGE
page 46

SAUVIGNON BLANC &
POUILLY FUMÉ
page 60

3-SECOND BIOGRAPHY
KEVIN JUDD
Founding winemaker at Cloudy
Bay who produced 25 vintages
of its flagship Sauvignon Blanc

30-SECOND TEXT
Jane Parkinson

The difference in Marlborough's day and night temperatures provides optimum conditions for growing Sauvignon and other aromatic white grapes – Riesling, Pinot Gris, Gewurztraminer and Grüner Veltliner – while Pinot Noir is the red grape of choice.

3-SECOND SIP
Marlborough is the region that put New Zealand wine on the map.

3-MINUTE TOP-UP
The price of Marlborough Sauvignon Blanc has been a hot topic recently following some very high-yielding vintages, which generated the nickname 'Savalanche' for the beginning of harvest. This volume drove prices down, and although this is being corrected, it was a bitter pill to swallow for a region and country that from the outset has commanded higher-than-average prices for its wine in general.

BAROSSA VALLEY
the 30-second wine

3-SECOND SIP
Barossa Valley is the engine room of Australia's most revered red wines, especially those made from Shiraz.

3-MINUTE TOP-UP
The terms Barossa Valley and Barossa are frequently and incorrectly used interchangeably. Barossa Valley wines are made exclusively from the valley's fruit, whereas wines labelled 'Barossa' can be a blend of grapes from Barossa Valley and its neighbouring region Eden Valley, which is famous for Shiraz and Riesling.

Less than 60 kilometres (40 miles) north-east of Adelaide, Barossa Valley is the powerhouse of Australia's top red wines. The vineyards, founded largely by German settlers from Silesia in Prussia are divided by the river North Para. In Barossa's hot and arid climate, Cabernet Sauvignon and Shiraz thrive. Old bush vines of Shiraz, some of them over a century old, impart an inimitable complexity to the wines on account of their great age, and are the reason for the deservedly iconic status and global reputation of Barossa Shiraz. The best of these wines are rarely at their drinking peak in youth, the sweet blackcurrant fruit, dense chocolate flavours and hefty tannins demand this wine is kept for a minimum of five years – and often more – before blossoming into perfect condition. Barossa Valley makes serious red wines from other Mediterranean varieties too, including Grenache and Mourvèdre (or Mataro in Australia) and when blended with Shiraz, formulate the popular GSM blended red wines. Semillon and Chardonnay are the most popular grapes used to make white wines, some of which can be as complex as the reds. Famous producers in this blessed region of South Australia include Penfolds, Wolf Blass and Jacob's Creek although the number of quality-obsessed boutique producers seems to be ever-increasing.

RELATED TOPICS
See also
RIESLING & SCHARZHOF BERGER
page 58

SYRAH/SHIRAZ & HERMITAGE
page 66

REGIONAL GRAPES & WINE STYLES
page 74

30-SECOND TEXT
Jane Parkinson

Australia's wine capital is one of its oldest winegrowing regions and perhaps the best-known new world wine region aside from California's Napa Valley. Barossa is synonymous with red gutsy wines, typically made from Grenache, Shiraz and Mourvèdre.

MENDOZA

the 30-second wine

Argentina's foremost wine region

lies in the rainshadow of the snow-capped Andes. Accounting for over two-thirds of Argentina's total wine production, Mendoza has adopted the French red-wine grape Malbec to such great effect that its name is almost synonymous with the country, despite the importance of other varieties, including Cabernet Sauvignon and Bonarda for red wines, and, for whites, Chardonnay and Sauvignon Blanc. (Torrontes, Argentina's signature white grape, is more at home in Salta than Mendoza.) Key to Mendoza's success are high altitude – crucial to temper the region's otherwise searing heat and provide a climatic (therefore wine) consistency from year to year – and drying winds off the Andes, which lessen the risk of moulds and rot. Thanks to a nineteenth-century French immigrant who first planted Malbec in Mendoza, this disease-prone, frost-sensitive grape happily took root under the Andes. The Uco Valley is currently one of Mendoza's most-heralded subregions, producing exquisite full-bodied Malbecs rich in black fruit and spice. Unusually, the valley is not named after a river but the person who introduced irrigation to this arid region. At its northernmost end, Tupungato is the subregion where some of Mendoza's best Chardonnay is produced.

RELATED TOPICS
See also
PHYLLOXERA
page 24

BORDEAUX'S RISE TO PROMINENCE
page 84

3-SECOND BIOGRAPHY
DOMINGO F. SARMIENTO
1811–88
Argentinian governor of San Juan who instructed a French agronomist to plant French vine cuttings in Mendoza

30-SECOND TEXT
Jane Parkinson

3-SECOND SIP
With over three-quarters of the world's acreage of Malbec, Mendoza has restored the grape as one of the top varieties for full-bodied red wine.

3-MINUTE TOP-UP
Mendoza's wine industry owes its success to the expertise of European immigrants escaping the scourge of phylloxera and to the skill of the indigenous Huarpe population, who created an intricate canal system that channelled the meltwater from the Andes, irrigating Mendoza sufficiently to grow grapes in a desert.

Mountain influences and bountiful sunshine mean Mendoza enjoys a long growing season (important for wine grapes to develop complexity of flavour), the fruit retaining fresh acidity while achieving optimum maturity.

September 1941
Born in Barcelona, Spain

1962
Graduates in Oenology
and Viticulture from
Dijon and takes over
at his family's winery

1966
Pioneers planting
international grape
varieties in Spain

1975
Begins experimenting
with organic viticulture

1977
Publishes his first book
Vines and Wines

1979
Torres' 1970 Gran
Coronas Reserva beats
Château Latour 1970
and a host of other top
Cabernet-based wines at
the Gault-Millau Wine
Olympiad in Paris

1979
Establishes Torres as
the first foreign wine
producer in Chile where it
now produces 4 million
bottles annually

1982
His sister Marimar plants
first US vineyard

1993
Marimar Estate Winery
opens in California

1996
Chilean Government
awards Torres Order of
Bernardo O'Higgins
(grado de gran oficial),
in recognition of his
contribution to Chile's
viticultural development

1997
Establishes joint
venture in China, the
Zhangjiakou Great Wall
Torres Winery Co. Ltd,
and a wholesale and
retail wine business,
Torres China

1999
Wine Spectator
magazine declares Torres
The Most Important
Winery in Spain

2001
Torres is the sole
Spanish winery listed in
Wine Spectator's 25th
anniversary Hall of Fame

2002
Named *Decanter*'s 'Man
of the Year'

2005
Named *Wine
International* magazine's
'Personality of the Year'

2006
Receives Lifetime
Achievement Award
from *Wein Gourmet*
magazine

2006
Torres named Best
European Winery by
Wine Enthusiast
magazine

2012
Fifth-generation Miguel
Torres Maczassek takes
over from his father as
Managing Director of
Bodegas Torres SA

2014
Torres named
World's Most Admired
Wine Brand by *Drinks
International*

MIGUEL A. TORRES

Miguel A. Torres is the fourth-generation President of a family-owned company founded by Jaime Torres in 1870 in Penedès, Catalonia. Miguel introduced to Spain modern vinification methods and grape varieties which transformed the image of Spanish wines abroad and made the Torres name synonymous with top-quality.

Miguel studied oenology and viticulture in Dijon, France, and joined the company in 1962 to embark on an impressive winemaking career driven by experimentation, innovation and achievement.

As early as 1966 he began to plant international varieties such as Chardonnay and Cabernet Sauvignon while remaining equally committed to Catalonia's little-known indigenous grape varieties. By 1970 he was using stainless steel tanks with temperature control to produce wines that were fresh, vibrant, fruity in style – revolutionary in Spain at the time. In 1975, ahead of the mainstream, he began experimenting with organic viticulture.

In 1979 the Torres name made headlines when, at the *Gault-Millau* Wine Olympiad in Paris, the Torres Gran Coronas Black Label 1970 (now called Mas La Plana), out-scored top Cabernet-based wines, including Bordeaux's Châteaux Latour and Haut-Brion.

That year Torres became the first foreign wine company to set up in Chile. Modern winemaking equipment and new oak barrels brought startling results which highlighted the country's potential and marked the start of a new era for Chilean wine. It is typical of Miguel Torres' ethical and forward-thinking character that he chose then to pay his Chilean workers four times the going rate, which he calculated to be the minimum required for a decent standard of living. Today Torres' Chilean winery is a certified organic and Fair Trade producer.

On the death of his father in 1991, Miguel became President and Managing Director. Today the company has wineries in several Denomination of Origin (DO) regions outside its native Penedès, including Priorat, Ribera del Duero, Toro, Jumilla and La Rioja as well as ventures in California and China. It spends ¤3 million a year on viticultural and winemaking research and has invested in higher, cooler vineyards in the foothills of the Pyrenees to mitigate effects of global warming and delay fruit maturation.

In the marketing of wine, he believes focusing on brand rather than region or grape variety is the most effective way to compete with New World producers. Fittingly, in 2014, Torres was named the World's Most Admired Wine Brand by *Drinks International* following a comprehensive industry poll of the world's best-regarded wines.

EMERGING ECONOMIES

the 30-second wine

A culmination of modern

influences – from outside investment to advanced technology – has placed the wines of emerging countries on the world's table. High on the list is Brazil, where historically high humidity meant the grapes grown were obscure hybrids that could withstand these inclement conditions. However, significant progress has been made in Brazil's top region, Rio Grande do Sul, especially with its most promising style to date: sparkling. Further north, and closer to the equator, is Vale do São Francisco, a source of fascination for growers in classic wine countries because here the semi-arid tropical conditions enable vines to produce two harvests a year. Across the Pacific, Asian countries too are improving wine quality, while determining the most suitable styles and/or grape varieties. Significant investment in China – for now more famous as a consumer than producer – combined with the arrival of foreign winemakers has endorsed its potential, in particular in Shandong province in the east and Ningxia in the west. In India, Maharashtra is currently the most productive wine region although wine production is flourishing everywhere thanks to government incentives, outside investment and a booming middle class eager to imbibe.

3-MINUTE TOP-UP
Growing grapes for wine on the American continent began in Mexico before spreading to Chile, Argentina and California. Spanish conquistadors took their love of wine to Mexico, which boasts the Americas' oldest winery, Casa Madero, founded in 1597. Until Mexico's independence, local demand was quenched with imports from Spain after Carlos II outlawed winemaking in the colony to protect the Spanish wine industry. Guadalupe Valley is widely tipped to be Mexico's hotspot for quality wine although styles vary greatly thanks to a melting pot of grape varieties.

RELATED TOPICS
See also
WINE INVESTMENT
page 136

30-SECOND TEXT
Jane Parkinson

Making wine is now a global industry and consumers accustomed to claret, California or Chilean wine are now able to sample the increasingly impressive output of countries without wine in their cultural tradition.

THE BUSINESS OF WINE

broker A middleman between wine growers and or merchants and customers. A broker may collect wine samples direct from the producer and present them to merchants, taking a small percentage of any sale. Fine wine brokers deal in fine and rare vintages selling wine to merchants and private customers. They may sell their own stock, typically still in its original wooden case under bond, or simply facilitate a sale between a seller and a buyer for a commission.

cave coopérative A cooperative winery owned by a group of local grape growers. They usually produce their own brands but also smaller *cuvées* for individual growers. Advantages include economies of scale and the opportunity for smaller growers, who might not otherwise be able to afford the winemaking infrastructure, to market their own wine.

caviste The French term for a specialist wine retailer.

courtier A French term for a broker who acts as a middleman between wine growers and or merchants and customers. A broker may collect wine samples direct from the producer and present them to merchants, taking a small percentage of any sale. A *courtier* often specializes in the wines of one region.

en primeur A wine trade term also known as pre-release. It refers to the selling of wine before it has been bottled and released to the market. It has been a traditional way for wine merchants to secure a share of a Bordeaux, Burgundy or Rhône vintage and in the late twentieth century the opportunity was extended to consumers. It is particularly popular in instances where demand is likely to exceed supply. The buyer pays the opening or 'cellar door' price and at some point, up to two years later, pays the shipping, duty and any applicable sales tax (such as VAT) before taking delivery of the wine. These days, en primeur markets exist around the world, wherever there is a perceived shortage of a particular wine.

evolution (of wine) Wine is constantly evolving. In the winery, the process can be slowed by storing newly made wine in an inert, air-tight, temperature-controlled stainless steel tank until bottling. Wines aged in barrels evolve more quickly due to greater exposure to air. Once bottled, wine has very little contact with air other than what is inside the bottle and the minuscule amount that enters through the cork over many years. Evolution in bottle is therefore anaerobic, especially if the bottle is sealed with an airtight Stelvin closure (screw cap). Fine wine often benefits from being allowed to evolve in bottle. White wines deepen in colour over time while red wines become lighter and the tannins soften. Primary characteristics such as fruitiness gradually give way to evolved, complex, nuanced flavours.

Ideal long-term cellaring conditions (1–50 years) are a cool, constant (12–14°C/53.6–57.2°F) temperature and a slightly humid environment free from direct light and vibration. Bottles should be laid horizontally to prevent the cork from drying out and the wine leaking.

First Growths The elite group of châteaux in the Médoc and Graves regions of Bordeaux ranked Premiers Crus in the official 1855 Classification. They are Châteaux Latour, Lafite-Rothschild, Mouton-Rothschild, Margaux and Haut-Brion.

flying winemaker One who makes wine in more than one country, typically a southern hemisphere vintage (January–March) followed by a northern hemisphere vintage (August–October). The term was coined by retail wine merchant Tony Laithwaite who, in the 1980s, brought in cutting-edge Australian and New Zealand winemakers to under-performing, old-fashioned and often unhygienic cellars in eastern Europe to raise standards and to make wine that would be more appealing to the British palate. The concept was taken up by other merchants and supermarkets, especially for own-brand wines, and became mainstream. Today's flying winemakers are just as likely to be European and found working in New World wineries.

in bond (IB) A wine held in a controlled warehouse and on which no duty has yet been paid. For investment purposes, fine wines often change hands many times while still in bond.

MW (Master of Wine) One who has passed the practical and written examinations held annually by the Institute of Masters of Wine. The MW is the wine trade's most demanding professional qualification. The first six MWs qualified in 1953. By 2014 there were still only 319 MWs worldwide. In many countries there are also official associations of sommeliers with their own qualifications such as Master Sommelier (MS). They also enter exams and competitions, not least one for the prestigious title of Meilleur Sommelier du Monde, World's Best Sommelier.

négociant The French term for a wholesale wine merchant who buys grapes, must or young wine in bulk from growers and then makes or blends and bottles it for sale under the négociant's wine label. Examples include Calvet in Bordeaux and Bouchard Père et Fils in Burgundy. Some négociants also make wine from their own vineyards.

PRODUCERS

the 30-second wine

Even though the word 'château' – or *schloss* or *castello* – is synonymous with fine wines, only a small proportion of modern wines comes from such properties. Bordeaux *châteaux* allocate production via trusted courtiers, who typically make 2 per cent on the sale. Courtiers allocate to négociants, who make 10–15 per cent. It's a complex web but ensures distribution is fair, and none can blame the Bordeaux *châteaux* if their allocation is modest. Most wine, though – particularly Burgundy – is made on the property by small growers, or domaines, producing a few thousand cases, enough to make a crust. Frequently, however, throughout France, Italy, Spain and elsewhere growers sell grapes, not wine. Often they are contracted to one winemaker who will specify vine-training techniques, yields, harvest times, etc. Much of Australia's production relies on such growers. Cooperatives, on the other hand, are owned by growers, perhaps numbering hundreds, who operate on terms such as grape variety and ripeness, not simply quantity. They can afford the equipment, oenologists and marketing muscle of which the lone grower can only dream, and many coops produce first-rate wines at modest prices.

RELATED TOPICS
See also
WINE INVESTMENT
page 136

3-SECOND SIP
From one-man bands to super-scale corporate businesses, wine producers – like wine bottles – come in all shapes and sizes.

3-MINUTE TOP-UP
The term 'estate bottled' and its equivalent '*mis en bouteille à la propriété*' (or '*au château*') indicate wine made and bottled on the estate by the grower – normally a superior product. Supermarkets' own-brands are frequently supplied by cooperatives, which offer consistently good quality, and many are a beacon of quality for their respective regions.

3-SECOND BIOGRAPHIES
BARON JAMES DE ROTHSCHILD
1792–1868
German-French banker, established the French branch of the Rothschild family

LOUIS GAMBERT DE LOCHE
1884–1967
French vineyard owner, founded the Rhône Cave de Tain co-op in 1933 and helped to establish appellation system

PETER LEHMANN
1930–2013
Australian producer who saved growers from ruin by buying grapes his employer had refused, establishing Barossa icon Peter Lehmann Wines

30-SECOND TEXT
Martin Campion

Fairytale castles feature in Bordeaux, the Loire, Rheingau and Tuscany; more widely producers are individuals or companies who dwell in ordinary houses.

BODEGA COOPERATIVA
CHESTE VINÍCOLA
1918

1931
CAVE COOPERATIVE
DE
MAREAU-aux-PRES
GROS & DETAIL

AGENTS, BROKERS & WINE MERCHANTS

the 30-second wine

RELATED TOPICS
See also
RETAILERS
page 130

WINE INVESTMENT
page 136

3-SECOND SIP
Two decades ago wine merchants were known for liking long lunches and Savile Row suits; today they are appreciated entirely for their business acumen, not their appearance.

3-MINUTE TOP-UP
Berry Bros. & Rudd, the archetypal traditional wine merchant, was established in London's St James's in 1698. With two royal warrants, leather-bound ledgers, even a letter from White Star Line confirming the loss of 69 cases on board RMS *Titanic*, one almost expects to hear the quiver of quill pens rather than the clatter of keyboards. Yet when its website launched in 1994 it was hailed as the Gold Standard and remains at the cutting edge of wine retailing.

In 2016, global wine production was 259 million hectolitres (57 billion gallons). Competition is fierce, and few producers have the resources to sell on a global scale. A top-notch agent who represents a winery beyond the local market is worth their weight in wine, developing detailed knowledge of customers' needs, responding to trends and allocating sought-after wines across myriad retailers and restaurants. Since the 1990s the significant rise in fine wine prices, and new wealth in countries such as Russia and China, has seen wine broking flourish. Wine brokers may act as importers for small, select producers, while simultaneously buying from, and selling to, fine wine enthusiasts. Many are active in the annual *en primeur* campaigns for Bordeaux and Burgundy – building a relationship with a broker can be the way to acquire a few precious bottles of a rare wine. A good merchant or wholesaler may combine all these roles: sourcing direct from hand-picked estates, buying from agents and brokers, and acting as brokers themselves, selling clients' wines to other clients, or to other brokers. In such a competitive market, it pays to establish an unique selling point (USP), such as Burgundy, California or Champagne.

3-SECOND BIOGRAPHIES
SIMON BERRY
1957–
Chairman of Berry Bros & Rudd and Clerk to the Royal Cellars

STEPHEN BROWETT
1959–
Chairman and owner of world-renowned wine-broker Farr Vintners, founded in 1978

30-SECOND TEXT
Martin Campion

Selling wine, like any other commodity, can be a local affair, conducted from the cellar door or, more likely, involve a chain of professionals to reach the global market.

RETAILERS

the 30-second wine

Fine wine is no longer the preserve of emperors, Oxbridge dons and the alumni of Harrow and Harvard: it is within the reach of ordinary people – so much so that in the UK, supermarkets represent 80 per cent of take-home sales. Retailers such as Waitrose have several MWs on their team and most have their own 'flying winemakers', whose experience and knowledge of customer preferences have helped to improve quality and drive sales. Frequently, they are spearheading wine-drinking trends. Tesco, one of the world's largest retailers, sells about 10 per cent of all Marlborough Sauvignon Blanc, and many, including US-based Costco, sell substantial quantities of Bordeaux Grands Crus at keen prices. Yet there remains room for the independent specialist, the lone *caviste*, whose *raison d'être* is not to compete on price, but to truffle out gems from small producers who hold little interest for volume-hungry supermarkets. London's Hedonism is a prime – perhaps extreme – example. With staff collectively speaking fifteen languages and a range of over 7,000 products, it has the lot: simple wines at a modest £8 a bottle to those requiring a banker's bonus, such as Krug 1966, Yquem 1811 and Penfolds 2004 Block 42 Ampoule – one of only twelve – a snip at £120,000 per bottle.

RELATED TOPICS
See also
AGENTS, BROKERS
& WINE MERCHANTS
page 126

WINE & FOOD
page 148

3-SECOND SIP
High-street retailers have changed the face of wine buying – and wine drinking – forever, placing wine alongside the weekly groceries.

3-MINUTE TOP-UP
Supermarkets often charge an artificially high price, only to slash it in a buy-one-get-one-free offer. Superficially this looks good for canny customers, but not for the humble grape grower. Few live in the opulent châteaux common to the élite of Bordeaux; fewer still can afford to turn down the supermarket looking for a deal. The result? Perfectly drinkable yet bland wines, made to please the purse more readily than the palate.

3-SECOND BIOGRAPHIES
JAMES SINEGAL &
JEFFREY H. BROTMAN
1936– & 1943–2017
American founders of Costco, one of the world's largest wine retailers, in 1983

TONY LAITHWAITE
1941–
English co-founder (with wife Barbara) of UK wine retailer Laithwaite's and the *Sunday Times* Wine Club

YEVGENY CHICHVARKIN
1974–
Russian mobile phone tycoon and founder of Hedonism Wines in 2012

30-SECOND TEXT
Martin Campion

Wine is now accepted as part of the culture in much of the westernized world.

SOMMELIERS

the 30-second wine

For long sommeliers had a

reputation for being lofty figures, steeped in fine wine since birth, and hardly the most approachable of restaurant staff. Dressed in a long black apron and black jacket, decorated with a silver or gold brooch shaped like a bunch of grapes to signify the wine connection, sommeliers could easily make diners feel uncomfortable or – worse – inferior when selecting wine. Fortunately, the profession has advanced considerably and diners now feel more freely able to talk to sommeliers, usually less sombrely dressed, about the wine(s) to accompany their meal, without risking humiliation. Sommeliers need to be versatile: their job encompasses far more than opening and serving wine. In order to describe and recommend a wine they must have extensive wine and food knowledge and be excellent tasters. However, they must also be commercially savvy to buy wines intelligently and price them well – competent sommeliers will be as adroit with accounting formulas and spreadsheets as corkscrews. And they require a healthy dose of psychology to capture the emotions of customers and understand correctly the type of occasion the diners are coming to experience. All that wrapped in a great sense of hospitality to ensure guests will return again and again to renew the pleasure.

3-SECOND SIP
The sommelier is the person charged with purchasing, recommending and serving wine in a restaurant.

3-MINUTE TOP-UP
Competitions to become the top sommelier exist at national, continental and international levels, including the truly global 'Best Sommelier of the World', and are avidly contested by large numbers of sommeliers. For long, sommellerie was a male-dominated trade, demanding unsociable hours and the regular manipulation of wine cases, but young women are increasingly assuming the role with great aplomb. A US documentary, *Somm* (2012), about the Master Sommelier examination, rapidly became a cult film.

RELATED TOPICS
See also
HOW TO TASTE
page 146

WINE & FOOD
page 148

3-SECOND BIOGRAPHY
PAUL BRUNET
1935–
French Master Sommelier, author and doyen of the sommellerie trade

30-SECOND TEXT
Gerard Basset OBE

Intimate knowledge of wine and food matches, professional service and a sense of occasion are the hallmarks of the top sommeliers.

WINE WRITERS, JOURNALISTS & CRITICS

the 30-second wine

'In vino veritas', Pliny the Elder famously remarked – 'in wine there is truth'. Pliny and fellow Roman Virgil wrote much on wine while Greek historian Thucydides referred to the civilizing effect of vine cultivation. Long after those ancient worthies first scribed on the topic, Edmund Penning-Rowsell, Pamela Vandyke-Price and Harry Waugh laid the foundations for modern wine-writing. For many, Hugh Johnson, author of the *Pocket Wine Book*, *The Story of Wine* and *The World Atlas of Wine*, is the greatest living wine writer, closely followed by fellow author, journalist and critic Jancis Robinson, whose website has global influence. Wine, like food, has become a standard feature of weekend newspapers and a glowing review can be enough to strip the supermarket shelves. *Wine Magazine* became the annual International Wine Challenge, while *Decanter* holds its World Wine Awards, both judged by winemakers, writers, sommeliers and buyers/sellers and a medal from either indicates a stand-out wine. *Wine Spectator*, which organizes yearly Fine Wine Encounters with the world's finest producers, holds significant sway in the USA. None has been more influential than the critic Robert M. Parker. For many, 100 points from RP are the holy grail, frequently guaranteeing a sellout vintage.

3-SECOND SIP
The public's thirst for knowledge is now quenched by an outpouring of wine publications and expert opinion.

3-MINUTE TOP-UP
First-century naturalist Pliny the Elder (23–79 CE) authored the 37-volume encyclopaedia *Naturalis Historia*; book 14 deals exclusively with wine, including a ranking of the First Growths of Rome, and book 17 includes viticultural techniques and the concept of terroir. In his ranking of the best Roman wines, he concludes the vineyard has more influence than grape variety on the finished wine, a view shared by most modern experts.

RELATED TOPICS
See also
TERROIR
page 16

WINE'S SPIRITUAL BEGINNINGS
page 80

RETAILERS
page 130

3-SECOND BIOGRAPHIES
HUGH JOHNSON OBE
1939 –
English author of international bestselling wine books

MARVIN SHANKEN MBA
1943 –
American publisher of the *Wine Spectator*

JANCIS ROBINSON MW OBE
1950–
English author of bestselling wine books, influential blogger and first non-wine trade MW

30-SECOND TEXT
Martin Campion

Wine books, blogs and column inches have done much to bring the noble beverage within the reach of ordinary people.

WINE INVESTMENT

the 30-second wine

3-SECOND SIP
Fine wine, like art, can be a good, relatively low risk, long-term investment.

3-MINUTE TOP-UP
Such has been Chinese interest in Bordeaux that, to paraphrase Victor Kiam's Remington ads from the 1980s, they bought the châteaux. It's estimated China had invested in over 60 properties by 2014, and not only in Bordeaux; in July 2014 a Chinese company 1847 Winery bought Château Yaldara in Australia's Barossa Valley. Investment flows in the other direction too; the Rothschilds of Lafite have planted over 25 hectares with Chinese partner CITIC, in the Penglai peninsula.

Obey a few simple rules and

investing in wine can be enormously rewarding. Buying *en primeur* guarantees provenance and allows buyers to select bottle sizes, though rare wines can be impossible to obtain without significant outlay on lesser wines, or substantial expenditure on other rarities. A case of top Bordeaux, such as 1990 Lafite could be bought for £400 *en primeur*, yet today stands around £10,000 at auction; the 1982 (cost £200) at nearly £25,000 (from a high of £42,000). Storing under bond saves money and guarantees the watchful eye of customs officials, which lessens the chance of the wine being a fake (a growing problem at auctions, though increasingly well policed). Bordeaux's dominance is diminishing slightly with top Burgundies soaring (2005 DRC has doubled to nearly £10,000 per bottle over the last few years) and other regions, such as Champagne and Italy's Piedmont, showing fine returns. Shrewd investors buy the best they can afford from a well-reputed merchant and store with a specialist such as world-renowned Octavian Cellars. If storing with the merchant, marking the investor's name quite literally on the case is the way to avoid them becoming one of many creditors in the event the merchant collapses.

RELATED TOPICS
See also
AGENTS, BROKERS & WINE MERCHANTS
page 128

WINE WRITERS, JOURNALISTS & CRITICS
page 134

ROBERT M. PARKER
page 138

3-SECOND BIOGRAPHIES
MICHAEL BROADBENT MW
1927–
English expert on wine, author and Head of Christie's Wine Department until 2009

SERENA SUTCLIFFE MW
1945–
English expert on Champagne and Bordeaux, author and Head of Wine at Sotheby's and former rival to Michael Broadbent on the London auction scene

30-SECOND TEXT
Martin Campion

It's wise to invest in what you enjoy: liquid assets are a palatable alternative to buying stocks and shares.

23 July 1947
Born Baltimore, Maryland

1967
Visits Alsace, his first introduction to French wines

1970
Makes his inaugural trip to the Rhône Valley

1973
Graduates in law from the University of Maryland

1978
Sends out complimentary issue of his wine journal, *The Baltimore/Washington Wine Advocate*

1983
Attracts wider attention following his resounding endorsement of Bordeaux's 1982 vintage, now acknowledged as one of the best of the century

1984
Retires from the Farm Credit Banks of Baltimore to devote himself entirely to writing his bimonthly *Wine Advocate*

1985
Publishes *The Wine Buyer's Guide to Bordeaux*

1986
Establishes, with his brother-in-law, Michael Etzel, a vineyard/winery in Oregon – Beaux Frères

1987
Publishes *The Wines of the Rhône Valley and Provence,* followed, in 1990, by *Burgundy*

1993
French President François Mitterrand makes him a Chevalier dans l'Ordre National du Mérite for services to French wine abroad

1999
French President Jacques Chirac promotes Parker to Chevalier dans l'Ordre de la Légion d'Honneur

1997
Publishes *Wines of the Rhône Valley* (2nd edn)

1998
Wine Advocate subscriptions reach 45,000 in 35 countries and the French language edition is launched

2002
Online version of erobertparker.com goes live. It is now the world's most-visited wine information website

2002
Made a Commendatore dell'Ordine al Merito della Republica Italiana) by Prime Minister Silvio Berlusconi for services to Italian wine

2006
Elin McCoy writes a biography, *The Emperor of Wine: The rise of Robert M. Parker, Jr, and the reign of American taste*

2011
Receives the Gran Cruz de la Orden del Mérito Civil), Spain's highest civic honour, from King Juan Carlos of Spain

2012
Appoints Lisa Perrotti-Brown as *The Wine Advocate*'s new editor-in-chief and sells his majority stake in the business to Singapore investors for $15 million

ROBERT M. PARKER, JR

From the late 1980s American wine critic Robert Parker dominated professional commentary on the world's most sought-after wines. Founder of the bimonthly review *The Wine Advocate*, he is also the author of several acclaimed books. He is known to prefer wines made in a ripe-tasting, opulent style and his pronouncements hold huge sway, especially with wine collectors.

Robert Parker grew up in rural Maryland. With no formal training in wine, his interest was sparked in 1967 while visiting the French region of Alsace. From then on he started tasting wines keenly and continued tasting widely and writing notes while studying law at the University of Maryland.

Back in the 1970s independent, impartial opinion on wine quality was not always easy to find, so in 1978, inspired by consumer activist Ralph Nader, Parker began publishing his own. Accepting no advertising, he vowed not be influenced by vested interests, history or tradition. His early, unconditional praise for Bordeaux's 1982 vintage, when others were more cautious, proved to be a huge turning point and slowly but surely raised his profile considerably at home and abroad. In 1984 he retired from law and worked long hours assessing up to 10,000 wines a year at the peak of his career.

Robert Parker is perhaps best known for his 100-point wine rating scale which, he maintains, permits 'rapid communication of information to expert and novice alike'. Top marks can instantly raise demand for, and the price of, individual wines and Parker points®, as they are known, are now routinely used as a promotional tool by wine trade professionals.

Critics of this system include British wine-writer Hugh Johnson, who posits that wine does not lend itself to such rigid numeric assessment. Others claim that some producers actively target high scores by altering their wines to appeal to Parker's tastes, a phenomenon referred to as the 'Parkerization' of wine.

Although Robert Parker may divide opinion, it is widely accepted that he has made fine wine more accessible to a new generation of consumers. In recognition of his services, he has received some of the highest civic honours from the governments of France, Italy and Spain.

In 2006 he began delegating the coverage of various wine regions to trusted members of his staff – although he remains active, continuing to insure his nose in 2008 for $1 million dollars – only relinquishing editorial control in 2012.

ENJOYMENT OF WINE

balance The overall harmony brought by the flavour and textural elements of a wine. A sweet wine requires acidity, a tannic red, a certain amount of ripe fruit. If any one element stands out, such as excessive alcohol or searing acidity, a wine is deemed to be unbalanced.

blind tasting An objective form of wine tasting in which participants assess the quality of a wine, and in some instances try to determine its precise origin without knowing its identity. Its prime benefit is to eliminate prejudices surrounding price, name and region.

cork taint A wine fault caused by a cork contaminated with trichloranisole (TCA), which causes the wine to smell mouldy and stale. It develops during manufacture as a result of cork bark being treated with a chlorine solution which reacts with the phenolics in the cork. In recent years new processes have reduced the incidence of taint which, at its height, was thought to have affected around one in 20 bottles.

dry A technical term that denotes a wine with little or no residual grape sugar. Often a wine has a ripe fruit flavour that suggests a degree of sweetness despite it being technically dry.

The French Paradox A term coined in the USA in 1991 in an attempt to explain statistical evidence that the French recorded a comparatively low incidence of coronary heart disease despite consuming larger quantities of saturated fats and units of alcohol per capita than most other nationalities. Red wine was cited as a possible influencing factor.

horizontal tasting A tasting of a number of wines from the same vintage, usually for purposes of comparison. By contrast, a vertical tasting is a tasting of different vintages of the same wine, usually also for purposes of comparison.

residual sugar The amount of grape sugar left in a wine after fermentation. Anything less than 3 grams per litre will taste completely dry.

table wine The internationally accepted term to describe still wines of average alcoholic strength (around 9°–15° by volume) as distinct from fortified wines. Table wines derive their alcohol naturally during fermentation while fortified wines have been strengthened by the addition of a neutral-tasting alcoholic spirit. Within the EU however, table wine has further connotations, being the most generic and undemanding quality wine category. Table wine translates as follows: France, *vin de table*; Italy, *vino da tavola*; Spain, *vino de mesa*; Portugal, *vinho de mesa*; and Germany, *tafelwein*.

TASTING TERMS

Words that form part of the wine taster's lexicon that help describe the characteristic colour, aroma and taste of a wine. While many words are immediately and universally understood, others pertain specifically to wine tasting and cannot therefore be taken literally. Here are some of the more common tasting terms that may require explanation.

APPEARANCE

core The centre of a glass of wine when held and tilted away from the taster.

rim The pale, sometimes watery-looking edge of a glass of wine when held and tilted away from the taster.

legs/tears The transparent strands of alcohol that run down the sides of a glass after swirling it or drinking from it. The higher the wine's alcoholic strength, the more noticeable the legs.

mousse A French term used to describe the fizziness of a freshly poured glass of sparkling wine.

SMELL

aroma An individual scent, such as berries or vanilla, that forms part of a wine's overall bouquet.

bouquet The sum total of a wine's aromas.

clean The aroma of a wine with no obvious faults.

TASTE

attack The very first impression a wine makes upon entering the mouth.

length The amount of time the flavour of a wine persists on the palate after swallowing or spitting.

finish The final impression left by a wine after swallowing or spitting. Often qualified by words such as 'smooth', 'long', 'persistent', 'aromatic' or 'dry'.

AGEING WINE

the 30-second wine

RELATED TOPICS
See also
SWEET WINES
page 42

FORTIFIED WINES
page 44

ÉLEVAGE
page 46

30-SECOND TEXT
Jane Parkinson

3-SECOND SIP
Good wine is worth keeping and great wine is built to last; it pays to store it well and reap the rewards when it reaches its peak condition.

3-MINUTE TOP-UP
In the last 25 years, Sotheby's have conducted four auctions of wines recovered from a famous collection of wines once owned by Nicholas II, the last tsar of Russia, from the Massandra Winery at Yalta on Ukraine's Black Sea coast. Preserved in deep tunnels in Crimea under Stalin's orders, hundreds of bottles survived, some over 150 years old, and included Madeiras, ports and locally produced Muscats.

Wines are typically aged for two reasons: to wait for the perfect drinking window and/or to appreciate in value. Wines bought for investment will maintain their best possible price if kept in professional storage facilities as the correct storage environment is crucial for controlling maturation. Key criteria include: a dark place to protect the wine from ultraviolet rays, constant temperature (preferably 10–14°C/50–57.2°F), and humidity (ideally 50–70 per cent) and laying bottles horizontally, to ensure the corks do not dry out. The least common style to be aged are dry white table wines, being lighter in structure, although those made from Chardonnay, Chenin Blanc, Riesling and Semillon are capable of long life. Top-quality dessert wines that are high in sugar such as Tokaji and Sauternes can age for decades. Fortified wines also possess the structure to age magnificently, especially port and even more so Madeira, which can keep for a century or more. Dry red table wines, made from grapes with abundant acidity and high levels of tannin, provide the framework for successful ageing, although maturation in oak barrels also contributes to higher tannins. Some of the world's most revered reds require patience: Bordeaux, Burgundy, Rioja, Napa Cabernet Sauvignon, the Super Tuscans and Barolo.

Many fine wines are built to last and, unlike most perishable goods, improve in quality over years or decades if the conditions are right.

HOW TO TASTE

the 30-second wine

Wine is usually consumed without being subject to scrutiny, but professionals – winemakers, sommeliers, buyers and journalists – and enthusiastic amateurs take an analytical approach to wine through the process of tasting, which begins with sight. A wine can be clear or cloudy (not necessarily a fault as unfiltered wine can be cloudy and perfectly fine), its colour hints at both grape variety and age while the 'legs' indicate a high sugar and/or alcohol content. On the bouquet, the most common fault is cork taint – caused by a biological reaction between the wine and mould inside the cork. Recognizable aromas and flavours on the nose and palate can imply grape variety, oak and the wine's origin. A mouth-puckering effect – the result of a wine with high acidity – can suggest cooler climates, grapes that have been picked early and/or grapes naturally high in acidity. Sweetness comes in varying degrees, from none for dry wines to intensely luscious for super-sweet wines, while tannin – the sometimes textured mouthfeel – commonly derives from contact with the grape skins during fermentation and possibly with oak during maturation (if wine is aged in new oak). Before tasting, professionals avoid anything that can weaken their palate – coffee, chocolate or toothpaste – or overpower a wine's delicate aroma – such as wearing perfume or aftershave.

RELATED TOPICS
See also
CLOSURES
page 48

AGEING WINE
page 144

3-SECOND SIP
Professional tasters undertake a sensory evaluation of a wine based on appearance, aroma, flavour, body, complexity, finish and overall quality.

3-MINUTE TOP-UP
'Vertical' is the name given to a tasting that comprises the same wine from a range of vintages whereas 'horizontal' refers to a tasting of different wines from the same vintage. 'Blind' tasting is the most intense form of tasting and involves providing no information about the wine, including covering its label.

3-SECOND BIOGRAPHY
MAXIMILIAN RIEDEL
1977–
Eleventh-generation member of the Austrian family that has manufactured crystal wine glasses since 1756

30-SECOND TEXT
Jane Parkinson

Tasting determines the various facets of a wine's character and is far more than a simple 'Do I like this?' test.

WINE & FOOD

the 30-second wine

Matching wine and food is

subjective to some degree. However, a few
practical guidelines are worth bearing in mind to
avoid any clash of combinations. Pairing rich food
with rich wine, for example, is one useful method
to follow. Conversely, contrasting wine and food
can provide excellent results, such as light crisp
white wine to cut through oily fish. One easily
understood principle is to match food with wine
from the same area because generations of
association with local produce reveal natural
affinities between regional specialities. Common
sense is often all that need apply: rich meaty dishes
are always going to be natural partners for bold
reds such as Barolo or Shiraz; or pink seafood with
dry rosé. Pinot Noir, incidentally – and usefully –
is one of the most versatile food-matching grapes
around. Cheese is a minefield as there are so many
different types. Historically, red wine was favoured,
but today white is increasingly served with some
cheeses as its inherent freshness counteracts
the high fat content. Here too there are regional
precedents such as chalky goat's cheese with crisp
Sauvignon Blanc, both products of Sancerre on
the Loire, or Comté cheese from the limestone
hills of the Jura with *vin jaune*, the local speciality
made from the Savagnin grape grown in this
region of eastern France.

RELATED TOPICS
See also
REGIONAL GRAPES & WINE
STYLES
page 74

SOMMELIERS
page 132

30-SECOND TEXT
Jane Parkinson

3-SECOND SIP
Choosing similar styles of
wine and food and balancing
their complementary
flavours are among the
best ways to ensure a
harmonious match.

3-MINUTE TOP-UP
Because the countries
of origin of spicy foods
often do not have a
wine-drinking culture,
matching remains a work
in progress. That said,
aromatic, fruity and
low-alcohol wines
consistently prove
themselves to work
well with spice, while
wines that are high in
tannin or alcohol are
best avoided.

*Enjoying wine with
food is a matter of
personal preference and
taste, but some flavours
and styles definitely
bring out the best in
each other.*

13 April 1902
Born George Philippe de Rothschild in Paris

1922
Placed in charge of Château Mouton Rothschild

1924
Decrees that all wine should be Château-bottled. Commissions a label by artist Jean Carlu featuring the words 'mise en bouteille au Château'

1926
Builds the spectacular, Charles Siclis-designed Grand Chai

1929
Racing his own Bugatti T35C he comes fourth in the Monaco Grand Prix

1930
Creates Mouton Cadet to market wine deemed of insufficient quality for an official Mouton Rothschild vintage

1932
Produces the film *Lac-aux-Dames*, the first French 'talkie' to achieve international recognition

1933
Establishes the wine négociant business, Baron Philippe de Rothschild SA in Pauillac

1933
Purchases Fifth Growth Château Mouton d'Armailhacq (renamed Château d'Armailhac in 1989)

1934
Marries Elisabeth Pelletier de Chambure

1941
Joins the Free French Forces of General Charles de Gaulle, later earning a Croix de Guerre medal

1945
Commissions original label artwork from Philippe Jullian, to commemorate the allied victory. The wine label has featured original artwork every year since

1954
Marries his mistress Pauline Fairfax Potter

1962
Opens the Museum of Wine in Art

1970
Purchases the neighbouring Fifth Growth Château Clerc Milon

1973
Mouton is elevated to Premier Cru Classé status, following a decree signed by Jacques Chirac, Minister of Agriculture

1979
Creates Opus One with California's Robert Mondavi, the first Franco-Californian ultra-premium wine, 'planted, made, matured and blended in the traditional Bordeaux manner'

20 January 1988
Dies in Bordeaux aged 85

BARON PHILIPPE DE ROTHSCHILD

Grand Prix racing driver, French freedom fighter, film producer, art collector, poet, playwright and playboy, Baron Philippe de Rothschild was a universal man. Above all, however, he was the protagonist in the story of Bordeaux wine in the twentieth century.

In 1922 the young Baron was put in charge of his family's wine property, Château Mouton Rothschild, where he had spent many happy years as a teenager during the First World War. It had always rankled him that in Bordeaux's famous 1855 Classification, Mouton had not been deemed a Premier Cru or 'First Growth' when the market price suggested it ought to have been. He vowed one day he would overturn this 'injustice'.

In the 1920s it was still common practice for wines to be shipped in barrel and bottled abroad. Unscrupulous merchants would sometimes 'stretch' supplies of great wine by blending them with *vin ordinaire*. Baron Philippe deemed that vintages should be bottled at the Château in order to guarantee quality and authenticity. Other estates soon followed suit.

The move also presented marketing opportunities. For the 1924 vintage he commissioned graphic artist Jean Carlu to design an art deco label, sending shock waves through conservative Bordeaux. The daring concept was re-launched in 1945 and original, one-off labels have been the Mouton signature ever since. Artists include Dalí (1958), Miró (1969), Chagall (1970), Picasso (1973), Warhol (1975), Prince Charles (2004) and Xu Lei (2008).

To maintain impeccable standards, Baron Philippe did not release the disappointing 1930 vintage as Mouton Rothschild but as a brand he created and named Mouton Cadet. Over time, sourced from various Bordeaux vineyards, it became the region's biggest seller.

In 1962 he opened the world-class Museum of Art in Wine in the estate's former barrel hall but the Baron's crowning achievement came in 1973. After 40 years of tireless campaigning, Mouton Rothschild was elevated to Premier Cru Classé. This caused much consternation among the Bordeaux establishment and no change to the sacrosanct 1855 classification has been made since and it is highly probable it never will be changed again.

In 1979, recognizing the great potential of New World wines, he embarked on a joint venture with California's Robert Mondavi, launching the Napa Valley's first super-premium wine, Opus One. Right up until his death in 1988, Baron Philippe remained a maverick and trendsetter, one of the most influential figures in wine, in Bordeaux and beyond.

WINE & HEALTH

the 30-second wine

Wine and health is no modern

issue, dating back as far as ancient Greece with the physician Hippocrates famous for believing wine to be an integral part of a healthy diet. Today, reports on the benefits or perils of drinking wine are endlessly debated, and although some are dismissed more quickly than others, one of the most enduring dates from the late twentieth century. The French Paradox observed the low incidence of coronary heart disease among people living in the south of France despite their notoriously rich diet, leading researchers to suggest red wine was the cause of this anomaly. Red wine is often cited as the most health-inducing style of wine because it is high in anthocyanins which contain powerful antioxidants. One of these, resveratrol, occurs in grape skins and vine leaves, and because red wine production typically involves longer contact of the juice with the skins, more resveratrol is extracted in making red wine than white. It's a widely held belief that the darker a wine's colour, the higher its antioxidant content although some authorities consider climate to be important in determining the levels of resveratrol in a grape, suggesting that grapes from cooler, wetter regions contain higher levels of resveratrol than those from hot and arid conditions.

RELATED TOPICS
See also
SULPHUR DIOXIDE
page 34

MAKING RED WINE
page 38

30-SECOND TEXT
Jane Parkinson

3-SECOND SIP
Drunk in moderation, red wine is widely believed to be the most beneficial wine style for one's health because of its high level of antioxidants.

3-MINUTE TOP-UP
Governments around the globe are under constant pressure to warn the public of the health effects of alcohol. Many release advice on how frequently it is drunk and the quantity that should be drunk, fervently supporting moderate consumption, because binge-drinking is considered harmful to health. Despite its wine-drinking culture, France has one of the harshest laws, la Loi Evin, restricting the advertising of alcohol.

The benefits or otherwise of the amount and type of wine we drink continues to generate healthy debate and discussion; the antioxidant resveratrol is found in the skin of grapes, and its benefits continue to be studied.

RESOURCES

BOOKS

Best White Wine on Earth:
The Riesling Story
Stuart Pigott
(Stewart, Tabori & Chang, 2011)

Bordeaux Legends
Jane Anson
(Stewart, Tabori & Chang, 2013)

The Grapevine: From the Science to the
Practice of Growing Grapes for Wine
Patrick Iland, Peter R. Dry & Tony Proffitt
(Patrick Iland Wine Promotions, 2011)

Inside Burgundy
Jasper Morris
(2010)

Inventing Wine: A New History
of One of the World's Most
Ancient Pleasures
Paul Lukacs
(W. W. Norton & Co., 2013)

Riesling Renaissance
Freddy Price
(Mitchell Beazley, 2004)

The Story of Wine
Hugh Johnson
(Mitchell Beazley, 2004)

Understanding Wine Technology
David Bird
(BBQA Publishing, 2010)

Venture into Viticulture.
Tom Crossen
(Country Wide Press, 2003)

Vintage: The Story of Wine
Hugh Johnson
(Simon & Schuster, 1989)

Viticulture: An introduction
to Commercial Grape Growing
for Wine Production
Stephen Skelton MW
(S. P. Skelton, 2009)

Viticulture Volume 1: Resources
B. G. Coombe & P. R. Dry (eds)
(Winetitles, 1998)

Viticulture Volume 2: Practices
B. G. Coombe & P. R. Dry (eds)
(Winetitles, 2006)

*Wine Science: The Application
of Science in Winemaking*
Jamie Goode
(Mitchell Beazley, 2014)

The World Atlas of Wine
Hugh Johnson & Jancis Robinson
(Mitchell Beazley, 2013)

Yquem
Richard Olney
(Flammarion, 2007)

MAGAZINES/JOURNALS

Decanter
decanter.com

Wine Spectator
winespectator.com

The World of Fine Wine
worldoffinewine.com

WEBSITES

Jancis Robinson's Purple Pages
www.jancisrobinson.com

NOTES ON CONTRIBUTORS

EDITOR

Gérard Basset OBE is currently the only person in the world to be given the combined titles of Master of Wine, Master Sommelier, Wine MBA and the World's Best Sommelier. Trained in Lyon, he became head sommelier at a Michelin-starred hotel in England and went on to co-found the Hôtel du Vin chain. Basset was honoured with the OBE in 2011 for services to the hospitality industry and named Man of the Year by *Decanter* magazine in 2013.

FOREWORD

Annette Alvarez-Peters is the principal buyer and director of wine for Costco, the sixth largest retailer in the USA.

CONTRIBUTORS

David Bird MW trained as an analytical chemist and entered the food manufacturing business as an analyst working with baby foods, mustard and fruit squashes. He moved into the wine trade in 1973 almost by chance, but in reality because a passion for wine was already developing. 1981 was his vintage year, becoming a Master of Wine, a Chartered Chemist and father to his first son. He specialises in quality assurance techniques, such as ISO 9000 and Hazard Analysis, and has been involved with wine activities in France, Italy, Spain, Portugal, Hungary, Denmark, Ukraine, Russia, Algeria, Australia and England.

Martin Campion has spent twenty-five years in the wine trade, working for Laithwaite's Wine and its sister companies. He is a passionate advocate for fine German Riesling, visiting many of the country's top producers every Spring to taste the new vintage and attending the VDP's September auctions, where most of the finest and rarest wines are sold. He lectures on Laithwaite's Wine and Spirits Education Trust programme and judges at the *Decanter* World Wine Awards, the International Wine Challenge and Meininger's Best of Riesling in Germany.

Jeremy Dixon first studied wine with the Australian Wine and Brandy Corporation in the 1980s before heading overseas to complete the WSET Diploma in London and the D.U.A.D at Bordeaux University's Institut d'Oenologie. His hands-on experience includes nine vintages as assistant winemaker in Theizé, Beaujolais. Today, a freelance commercial writer, he specialises in wine, food and travel for clients such as the Telegraph Group; works extensively for Laithwaite's and judges on occasions at the *Decanter* World Wine Awards.

Paul Lukacs is a professor of English at Loyola University, Maryland, and a wine writer with a special interest in wine history. A wine columnist in Washington, DC for nearly 20 years, he has won numerous awards for his work, and his books include *American Vintage: The Rise of American Wine* and *Inventing Wine: A New History of One of the World's Most Ancient Pleasures*.

Debra Meiburg MW is an award-winning author, TV personality, international speaker and a leading voice in wine education in Greater China. She was ranked the 7th most powerful woman in wine by the *Drinks Business* magazine. Debra is producer and host of several documentaries and TV shows, including *Taste the Wine* that is broadcast in 26 countries. She developed a suite of award-winning wine educational books and tools currently distributed on four continents as well as guides to the Hong Kong, Shanghai, Beijing and Singapore Wine Trades, firmly establishing her as a key voice for wine in Asia.

Jane Parkinson is an award-winning wine journalist and broadcaster. Recently awarded the International Wine & Spirit Competition Communicator of the Year 2014 title, she is a wine expert on BBC1 *Saturday Kitchen Live* and released her debut book *Wine & Food* in 2014. Jane is Wine Editor of *Restaurant* magazine, Wine Expert for *Stylist* magazine and one of five members of The Wine Gang. She regularly contributes to magazines and newspapers and discusses wine on radio and television. Jane is also a previous recipient of the Chairman's Award at the Louis Roederer International Wine Writers' Awards.

Stephen Skelton MW started his career in wine in 1975. After 12 months at Schloss Schönborn in Germany's Rheingau winegrowing region and two terms at Geisenheim Wine School, he returned to the UK in 1977 to establish Tenterden Vineyards in Kent (now the home of the UK's largest wine producer Chapel Down) where he made wine for 23 vintages. He was also winemaker at Lamberhurst Vineyards between 1988 and 1991. He became a Master of Wine in 2003 and won the prestigious Mondavi Prize. In 2005 he was awarded the AXA Millésimes award for his contribution to the work of the MW Education Committee. In 2014 he was elected to be Deputy Vice Chairman of the Institute of Masters of Wine. He also lectures on viticulture for Wine and Spirit Education Trust's Diploma courses. Stephen is a consultant to the English wine industry and is involved with planting vineyards for the production of both still and sparkling wines. Since 1986 he has written and lectured widely on English wine and has published four guides to UK vineyards, the 2001 edition of which won the André Simon award for 'Wine Book of the Year'. He has also written *Viticulture* a primer on the subject for students, and *Wine Growing in Great Britain* for growers.

INDEX

ACKNOWLEDGEMENTS

PICTURE CREDITS
The publisher would like to thank the following for
permission to reproduce copyright material:

All images from Shutterstock, Inc./www.shutterstock.com
and Clipart Images/www.clipart.com unless stated.

21:   Jamie Bush.
22:   Ivan Hissey.
27b: Tyson Kopfer/Cayuse Vineyards.
33:   Dr Jeremy Burgess/Science Photo Library.
41t: Eric Zeziola/Champagne Louis Roederer.
41b: Lordprice Collection/Alamy.
43t: Bon Appetit/Alamy.
43b: Craig Hatfield.
45tl: Gonzalez Byass.
45tr: Thomas Istvan Seibel.
46:   Kirsten Georgi.
50:   Roux Olivier/Sagaphoto.com /Alamy.
68:   Lacy Atkins/San Francisco Chronicle/Corbis.
85r: Philippe Roy/Hemis/Corbis.
85l: Interfoto/Sammlung Rauch/Mary Evans.
93tr: Champagne/Alamy.
94:   Nik wheeler/Alamy.
103: Stephanie Evans.
107: Library of Congress.
118: Bloomberg/Contributor.
121t: Clay McLachlan/Aurora Photos.
121r: Lou Linwei/Alamy.
129: Peter Wheeler/Alamy.
132: Alamy/Ian Shaw; OJO Images; Robert Kneschke.
135: Raymond Reuter/Sygma/Corbis.
138: Patrick Bernard/Stringer.
150: Charles O'Rear/Corbis.

All reasonable efforts have been made to trace copyright
holders and to obtain their permission for the use of
copyright material. The publisher apologizes for any
unintentional omissions in the list above and will gratefully
incorporate any corrections in future reprints if notified.